Ten Commitments for Building High Performance Teams

by
Tom Massey

Robert D. Reed Publishers • Bandon, OR

Robert D. Reed Publishers
P.O. Box 1992
Bandon, OR 97411
Phone: 541-347-9882 • Fax: -9883
E-mail: 4bobreed@msn.com
web site: www.rdrpublishers.com

Typesetter: **Barbara Kruger**
Cover Designer: **Grant Prescott**

ISBN 1-931741-53-0

Library of Congress Control Number 2004117588

Manufactured, typeset and printed in the United States of America

For those who aspire to leave the world a better place.

Contents

Introduction

Team performance is only as strong as the collective performance of its members. When committed, collaborative individuals with complementary skills work together, a synergistic effect takes place—total performance is greater than the sum of the individual parts. In other words, one plus one no longer equals two. Instead, it equals three or even more in a high performance team environment.

The ten commitments outlined in this book will help you get the right people in the right positions to develop a focused, values-driven, high performance team. Learn how to get every member to take personal ownership of your team's success by creating shared purpose, values, and strategic goals. Gain insights on setting up profit-sharing, establishing work standards, and correcting performance problems, in addition to creating a learning organization that is able to adapt to the challenges of the next century. Build a team environment where people have fun and play to win.

Here is a brief summary of the topics covered in each chapter:

❑ *Commit to getting the right people "on the bus."* Take the time and effort to clarify the skills and behavioral standards that each job requires, and identify cultural factors that influence performance, then hire the most qualified, enthusiastic, and committed people you can find.

❑ *Commit to getting everyone "on the same page."* By making a commitment to developing a common purpose and setting the ground rules for your team, you can ensure that expectations are aligned and there is a unified front to successfully engage any challenges.

❑ *Commit to creating a learning environment.* New and expansive patterns of thinking are nurtured as people are set free to aspire and create. In a learning environment, people see the whole picture together and are more flexible and adaptive to change. They are able to continually re-create themselves and soar higher.

❏ *Commit to sharing the profits and losses.* When people share both profits *and* losses, they take ownership of the team or organization. When your team reaps the rewards and assumes the risks of doing business, they will make a physical, emotional, and mental investment in quality performance.

❏ *Commit to turning around poor performance.* When a person's poor performance does not change, it creates problems for you, your team, and your organization. Your goal in correcting performance problems should be to positively influence future behavior and to build motivation for both the individual and the team.

❏ *Commit to dancing with "those that brought you."* Regardless of the services or products your team produces, people are your greatest asset. If you want people to be loyal to the team, then they must perceive loyalty in return.

❏ *Commit to playing to win.* If you want your team to reach levels of high performance, you must transform moments of fear and uncertainty into opportunities for ordinary people to achieve extraordinary results.

❏ *Commit to growing through adversity.* Adversity elicits talents and strengths that may have otherwise lain dormant. Help your team to deal with conflict head-on in order to find better solutions and develop a more solid foundation of trust.

❏ *Commit to having fun.* Having fun may be the single most important characteristic of a high performance team. Research indicates there is a positive correlation between fun on the job and employee productivity, creativity, and morale, as well as customer satisfaction and other factors that determine success. Make fun an integral part of your work culture, or better yet, make it one of your team's core values.

❏ *Commit to playing large.* If you want to move your team from being good to being great, shift your focus from merely the bottom line to the impact you are making in the lives of your team members, customers, and community. When team members are committed to purposeful outreach, they recognize greater value from their work, which increases their sense of commitment to the job and generates higher performance.

To assist you in applying the principles in the book, I have included a number of questions and activities at the end of each chapter. I suggest that you simply read the book straight through first to become mentally connected to the flow of ideas. Then read and apply a new chapter every week, every two weeks, every month, or in whatever time frame you choose. Knowledge is best learned by action. By putting the principles in this book into action, you will experience increases in team member retention, job satisfaction, commitment, and ownership at every level, as productivity rises to propel your team to a championship performance.

1.

Commit to Getting the Right People "on the Bus"

"Never doubt that a small group of thoughtful,
committed citizens can change the world;
indeed, it's the only thing that ever has."
—Margaret Mead

Fannie Mae was losing $1 million every business day in the mid-1980s when David Maxwell was selected to take the helm as CEO. The board desperately wanted to know what he was going to do to rescue their sinking company. "Give us the plan," they said, wanting to know exactly what he had in mind. Maxwell responded by telling them the correct first question should be "who" not "what." They had to get the right people on the bus before they decided where it was going.

Maxwell met with his management team and conveyed to them that there would only be seats on the bus for people who were totally committed to the success of the organization. He met with every member of the team, informing them that the trip would be demanding and he expected nothing less than total dedication and top performances from each. He told them if they didn't want to or felt that they could not commit to go under those circumstances, "the time to get off is now—with no questions asked." Out of 26 executives, twelve stayed on board the bus, each with tenacious determination and commitment to do what it took to turn the company around. Maxwell replaced the others with some of the brightest, most capable, and hard-working executives in the financial world.

With the right people on the bus, Maxwell and his new team could now turn their full attention to the "what" question. Their collaboration resulted in a plan of action that took Fannie Mae from losing $1 million a day to earning over $4 million a day! Furthermore, they generated cumulative stock returns that were eight times higher than the general market for the next two decades. That's high performance teamwork!

When you have the right people on the bus, with the right skills and a high-level commitment, regardless of whether you are a business manager or coach of a sports team, you will be successful.

Bill Hewlett and Dave Packard formed their partnership over 60 years ago, working together in a small house in Palo Alto, CA, beginning with $538 operating capital. Their first product was a resistance-capacity audio oscillator of which Walt Disney ordered eight to make the movie "Fantasia."

As Hewlett and Packard began to expand their business they felt that the direction they were headed was in the electronics industry. However, their primary objective from the inception was not to develop specific products, but to build an organization comprised of the right people making sure the work environment was conducive to creativity and growth. They knew that *the only way to grow a business is to grow people.*

They believed that once they had the right people on the bus, great products would be conceived and created. They were right. Hewlett Packard grew into a billion dollar company and remains one of the major players today in the computer and electronic industries throughout the world.

Develop Job Descriptions Based on Factors of Success

The first place to start when picking the right people for your team is to develop job descriptions based on factors of success for each position. I asked a group of business leaders recently whether or not they developed these factors for each of the positions for which they hired. Most of them responded that they only went to that "trouble" for manager or executive level people. I told them that was similar to a football coach getting the best skilled players to play quarterback and running back, while being satisfied with merely throwing in some "big guys" to do the blocking and tackling on the line. Could you imagine University of Southern California football coach Pete Carroll, arguably the best in the sport today, saying to his assistant coaches, "Guys, we need to make sure that we recruit All-American running backs, and by the way, let's get some wide bodies to play on the offensive line."

Great coaches and managers develop every position as if it is the most important position on the team, and it is.

Remember the adage: *A chain is only as strong as its weakest link.*

Factors of Success may be defined as:

The skills and behaviors needed to perform a job successfully within the culture the team operates.

These factors include more than simply the skills requirements. Skills requirements are essential characteristics or experiences every team member must have in order to qualify for their respective position. However, there are other behavioral standards required to ensure team success. For example, instead of saying the job requires "good communication skills," you should describe what the person can do because of those skills, such as "utilize listening and negotiation skills that result in a rating of 90% or higher on customer service feedback surveys."

When identifying success factors related to a position on your team consider the following three things:

- ❑ **What?**—Define what the person must do. Part of this will be defining specific job skills requirements.

❑ **How?**—Synthesize your understanding of the job to develop observable actions necessary for the person to complete in order to be successful in the job.

❑ **Where?**—Identify the culture in which the person must work.

Skills Requirements

When defining a position, you should first determine what the chief purpose of that job is and how it fits into the overall purpose of the team. <u>Each team member must see their position as a personal mission that contributes to the team's success.</u> Consider the following results of a recent national study involving over 20,000 employees in diverse industries:

❑ Only 37 percent of employees said they have a clear understanding of what their team or organization is trying to accomplish and why.

❑ Only 20 percent were passionate about their team's goals.

❑ Only 20 percent said they have a clear "line of sight" between their jobs and their team's goals.

In order to ensure that team members understand how their job contributes to the overall success of the team or organization, answer the following questions:

❑ What is the purpose of the job?

❑ What is the expected result or outcome of this position?

❑ When the job is performed well, what will be the benefit to the team member performing the task?

❑ When the job is performed well, what will be the benefit to the organization?

After identifying the purpose of the job and how it relates to the organizational goals, establish what skills and knowledge are necessary for a successful performance. Skills generally fall into the following categories: technical, problem-solving, or inter-personal. It is critical to define the essential characteristics or set of observable skills that each team member must possess in order to do the job. When you consider new candidates for a position, administer tests to observe their skills. Sometimes people look really good on paper, but you can only know how good they really are when you watch them perform.

Behavioral Standards

You must clearly define the major responsibilities and performance standards. People should clearly understand what constitutes an "outstanding job." Identify behavioral factors which may entail physical requirements, technical ability, or issues of personal character that are required on the job. These should be defined to be as measurable as possible so that they may be observed and evaluated.

Listed below are some examples of behavioral standards that may be required for a work position. An interesting note: You cannot ask someone on a job interview if they have a bad back or other physical impairments, but you can inform them that the job requires lifting 40 lb. boxes from a delivery truck and inquire if that will be a problem.

Examples of physical requirements: *Re specific*

- ❏ Lift 40 lb. boxes from a delivery truck and place on loading dock.
- ❏ Work rotating shift assignments or weekends.
- ❏ Stand for periods of two to four hours.

Examples of technical ability:

- ❏ Develop effective accounting procedures for reporting regional earnings and expenses.
- ❏ Create and maintain a database of customer contact information.
- ❏ Deliver dynamic sales and marketing presentations to customers.

*Ethical
Behabior*

Examples of personal character:

❏ Responsible for handling large sums of money.
❏ Get along with others and work well as a team player.
❏ Take initiative to be a self-starter with little direct supervision.
❏ Maintain a highly respectful public image at all times.

It is also important to identify the possibility of future changes in a position or performance expectations. For example, if you are planning to convert to a new accounting system in the next reporting period, the person you hire now may need to develop new skills required to use that system. The main point is there should be no surprises when it comes to making changes in the future.

Cultural Factors

Culture is defined as the norms of behavior that determine how work gets done in a team. How would you describe your work culture?

❏ Do positions require decision-making or problem-solving abilities with little supervisory direction?
❏ Is it necessary that each team member provide information to others to perform their jobs?
❏ Is the work pace constant or does it fluctuate between highly busy and slow periods?
❏ Do constant changes take place in the assignment of tasks?
❏ Is the work environment extremely hot or extremely cold?
❏ Are there constant deadline pressures?
❏ Are team members required to regularly deal with difficult or irate customers?

One of the big issues in the sports world today is the issue of players responding, sometimes violently, to difficult home-team fans. I recently watched a brawl disguised as a basketball game on television. While I don't think that buying a ticket to get in should give an attendee a permit to abuse players, fans should be expected to be loud, enthusiastic, and distracting for visiting players. It is part of the culture, so coaches and players must learn to deal with it in a productive manner. They must talk about it and prepare a plan of action to respond when fans, or opposing team members, become rowdy. These are the types of cultural factors that should be identified and discussed when selecting team members.

Choose Character First

A business manager once mused to me, "Why is it that we always seem to hire for skill, yet fire people because of character issues? Why not hire for character to begin with?"

Why not hire for character first? Is it too difficult to judge character or are we simply willing to overlook it to get someone who is really skilled at their position? And what does this oversight cost the team? Plenty—in terms of team morale and a public image that sometimes becomes tarnished.

If you are not currently conducting background checks on prospective team members, I emphatically recommend it. Due to federal statutes that arose in the 1990s, employers may now be generally held liable for the criminal or violent acts of their employees that occur outside the workplace, after working hours, or outside the course and scope of employment. Therefore, it has become critical to conduct pre-employment background checks before offering jobs to applicants. Additionally, if you as an employer fail to take appropriate disciplinary actions for existing employees in the form of retraining, reassignment, or termination, then you could also be legally liable. You have a legal duty to select fit and competent employees, in addition to retaining employees with a conscious regard for the rights and safety of others.

The cost of a basic package for background checks ranges from $25 to $100 per search and the turnaround time is typically twenty-four to seventy-two hours. On a practical basis, this practice will help you:

- Reduce turnover
- Enhance security in the workplace
- Minimize disciplinary issues
- Make hiring decisions less stressful

A basic search will typically investigate an applicant's criminal history, motor vehicle report, and social security verification. Additionally, searches may include:

- ❑ A credit report
- ❑ Education verification
- ❑ License verification
- ❑ Military records verification
- ❑ Workers' compensation filings
- ❑ Sexual offender/child molester identification

You may wonder why it would be necessary to perform a credit check for prospective employees. Let me respond with a question to you as a business owner or manager: *If a person does not manage their own resources in a responsible manner, would you trust them to manage yours?*

If you are a college coach you may not be able to perform the same type of background check for students that employers do for employees. However, you can make inquiries about the player's character to former coaches, teachers, and teammates that will help identify patterns of behaviors that may be detrimental to your team.

I'm not saying that people should always be written off for making mistakes. History is full of success stories about people who were given second, third, and even fourth, chances to redeem themselves. By conducting character checks you can at least become aware of potential pitfalls and help set boundaries that will help to avoid problem behavior.

Occasionally standards of behavior are paradoxical. Consider the defensive linebacker who makes 16 unassisted tackles, is cheered on by 100,000 fans and receives the game's Most Valued Player award, then, after the game, uses the same, take-no-prisoners tenacity that he was applauded for hours before, to beat the living you-know-what out of three fraternity guys at a party. Or that top salesman who has been repeatedly rewarded for his aggressive never-take-no-for-an-answer approach in setting sales records, while being seen as an overbearing jerk by his co-workers when displaying the same type of aggressive behavior in the office.

On one hand we applaud the behavior on the playing field, while we cringe or even reprimand when the same behavior is exhibited in other arenas of life.

This type of behavior can become a major distraction and a hindrance to your entire team's performance. You can reduce these circumstances by ensuring that each member of your team completely understands the boundaries for appropriate behavior and has the self-discipline to be personally accountable for his or her own character.

The problem with character today is that people try to make it relative to what others are doing — "But, but, look at what they did! I wouldn't have done what I did if they hadn't done that. It's their fault."

Character is *not* relative. What if your accountant professed to you that he is relatively honest? Would you trust that person to handle your money? Each member of your team must clearly understand and be willing to practice personal accountability for their actions — without excuses.

Hire for Enthusiasm and Commitment

I once saw a television news documentary about a traffic policeman in a large metropolitan area. He directed traffic at one of the busiest intersections in the city, where, during the rush hour, lines of cars moved at a snail's pace. It was interesting to observe the facial expressions change as drivers approached the officer — transformed from irritation to delight. This guy didn't merely direct traffic, he put on a show. Many drivers would actually pull over into nearby parking lots just to watch him perform.

He danced, twirled, waved his arms wildly, and shuffled his feet rhythmically through the intersection. He could moon walk and direct traffic at the same time! It was obvious that he was enthusiastic about his job. He didn't just show up for work every day, simply going through the motions. He was genuinely excited to be there. This is who you want on your team — a person who is excited about being there. When you hire someone whose enthusiasm intersects with the job, they will do a great job with little or no supervision.

Hire tough and manage easily. By taking the time and effort to clarify skills and behavioral standards that each job requires and identifying cultural factors that influence performance...then hiring the most qualified, enthusiastic, and committed people you can find...you will ensure that the right people are on the bus headed toward a championship performance.

Practical Application

1. Are you currently developing job descriptions with success factors including background checks to get the right people in the right positions on your team?
2. Begin with one position that needs to be filled now or in the future and develop a job description based on all success factors. Solicit feedback from key stakeholders who may be affected by this position: supervisors, peers, customers, etc. Include skills requirements, behavioral standards, and cultural factors that affect this position.
3. Use the Success Factors Profile as a worksheet to plan the interviews and evaluate job candidates.
4. The following people should be involved in the interview process for potential job candidates: 1) the manager or supervisor to whom the new employee will directly report; 2) a team leader or peer(s) who will be working with the new employee; 3) an H.R. professional should also be included to help establish interview questions that comply with Equal Employment guidelines.
5. Repeat step 2 for every position on your team.

open positions

2.

Commit to Getting Everyone "on the Same Page"

"Change without principle is chaos;
change based on principle is progress."
—Dwight Eisenhower

In late Spring, 1787, guards stood at the door of the Pennsylvania State House to protect the men inside from the sound of passing carriages and to keep curious onlookers at a distance. George Washington was nominated for the presidency of the Constitutional Convention and elected unanimously. With modesty, the General expressed his embarrassment at his lack of qualifications to preside over such a distinguished body and apologized in advance for any errors that might befall him during the course of its deliberations.

This began a difficult, yet worthwhile, process of establishing the ground rules by which this nation would conduct future business. Up until then, there was little power to regulate commerce by a central government. It could not tax and was generally ineffective in setting commercial policy. It could not effectively settle quarrels between states. Due to this weak national coalition, the states were on the brink of economic disaster and the evidence was overwhelming. Congress was attempting to function with a depleted treasury. Paper currency was flooding the country, creating extraordinary inflation—a pound of tea in some areas cost as much as $100. The depressed condition of business was taking its toll on small farmers. Many were being thrown into jail for debt, and numerous farms were confiscated and sold for taxes. Chaos ran rampant. The leaders desperately needed to get everyone on the same page if they were to move the country forward with success.

James Madison, a small, boyish-looking, 36-year-old delegate from Virginia, had the answer. What the country needed was a strong central government operating by a set of shared principles that would provide order and stability. Thus Madison, along with others, including a young lawyer from New York named Alexander Hamilton, began the grueling and often frustrating process of repeatedly drafting and revising the document that was to become the Constitution of the United States of America.

By late 1791, three-fourths of the states had ratified the Constitution, comprised of the ten amendments now well known to Americans as the "Bill of Rights." Many of the delegates left Philadelphia with doubts that the Constitution outlined the ideal form of government for the country, but James Madison declared, "No government can be perfect. That which is the least imperfect is therefore the best government."

This brief history lesson exemplifies the fact that any time a group of people comes together for a united cause there should be a common purpose and a set of shared rules by which they will conduct business. It doesn't work well to have everyone making up their own rules, as the founders of our country discovered. It will eat away at stability and productivity. *Even in their imperfection, some rules are better than no rules.*

Established rules provide structure. People know what is expected of them and how they will engage one another in day-to-day interactions. Conflicts commonly arise in teams because of failed expectations caused by assumptions of one of more people. These assumptions often result from implicit agreements or standards of behaviors that have not been clarified because people don't understand the rules of engagement.

Create a Team Charter

A team charter is a written document used to define the team's purpose/vision, values, and strategic goals. The charter will also help to:

- ❏ Serve as a contract between the team and the organization it represents.
- ❏ Define the work effort and its intended results to avoid redundancy or "gaps."
- ❏ Keep the team focused and evaluate whether its activity meets an expected standard.
- ❏ Define boundaries and help team members determine when to re-negotiate if necessary.

Charters may be developed by top management, then presented to team members, or teams can create their own charters and present them to top management. Regardless of who creates the charter, it is absolutely imperative that top management give their full endorsement to provide the team the direction and authority it needs to succeed. Teams need to know what top management expects of them, but just as important is the idea that top management needs to know what the team expects of them.

Develop a Purpose Statement

The team charter generally begins with a Purpose Statement, a one or two line statement explaining why the team is being formed. The purpose statement should align with and support the organization's mission. This statement should be succinct and simple enough for each member to commit to memory.

Here are some examples of purpose statements:

- ❏ To manage an annual fund-raising campaign in a cost-effective manner on behalf of the health and human service needs of Johnson County.
- ❏ To serve as a central resource for the recruitment, training, and deployment of quality employees for Smith Company.
- ❏ To provide quality technical assistance and computer training to the staff and faculty of East Central University.

Identify Team Values and Ground Rules

Values should define the core priorities and codes of conduct for the team. They are extremely important for strategic planning because they will drive future decisions and objectives. High performance teams are values-driven.

Values clarification is most effective when team members arrive at their own identification. Recent industrial surveys show employees often do not believe the value statements their company professes because they don't see those values being acted out by top management. Real values must be internalized and put into action by *everyone* on the team.

The foundation on which all high-performing teams is built is trust. In order to build trust people must have respect. Respect for all stakeholders—team members, customers, and community—must in some way be reflected within the four to six core values from which the team is to operate.

Here are some examples of value statements:

❑ We value and respect each member for his or her individual contribution to the team.

❑ We commit to excellence and quality performance to promote team success.

❑ We believe that employees have the right to know the essence of our business and should be given the opportunity to provide input.

❑ We value knowledge and are committed to continuous learning through providing regular staff training and mentoring opportunities.

❑ We commit to the promotion of self-esteem and self-respect.

❑ We believe in accomplishing our goals through a unified team effort.

❑ We commit to create a work environment that provides fun, meaningful work for each team member.

Notice that each value statement begins with words such as "we value," "we believe," or "we commit." These should serve as public affirmations for the rules upon which you will conduct business. After identifying your values, specify in some way how these values will be put into action.

Besides serving as a set of ground rules for your team members, value statements can serve as a guide for making strategic planning decisions. Before making future plans, always check your values first and ask the question, "Can we do this without compromising what is most important?" Remember to keep the main thing the main thing.

For example, say you plan to grow your business by twenty percent in the next year, which is a perfectly legitimate expectation. What do you need to do to increase your organization's infrastructure to accommodate the growth without compromising the quality of your products and the quality of experience for your work team? I have often seen organizations grow too rapidly only to sacrifice product quality and cause employees to suffer burn-out because of overwhelming workloads. This type of practice may have negative long-term consequences on your business.

Develop S.M.A.R.T. Strategic Goals/Objectives

Strategic goals and objectives should clearly state what a team is going to attempt to achieve — a target for people to shoot for and become excited about. Write your goals with the acronym S.M.A.R.T. in mind:

❏ **S**pecific — Each goal should name exactly the final product or action to be taken, along with the expected quality of the outcome.

❏ **M**easurable — You should be able to determine whether the outcome has been achieved through measuring, counting, weighing, or observing.

❏ **A**ttainable — The team should reasonably have the ability or resources to accomplish the goal.

❏ **R**elevant — Each goal should be congruent with the team's values. If the team doesn't value the outcome, how much enthusiasm do you think it will generate? And if goals are

not connected to core values, individuals and teams may not
muster the discipline to achieve them.
- ❏ **T**ime Driven—A definite date or time should be defined for
the completion.

Spend time initially thinking about the team when developing
goals and objectives. What are the problems it faces? What
processes need to be put into place for improvement? What are the
development needs and requirements of members?

Decide upon what action is desired. What will be the results of
that action? How does it fit in with your values and how does it
benefit the team?

Think about measuring the work you are about to specify. Draft
some measurable standards that must be met and identify how you
can tell whether or not those standards were met. What will be the
measure of results in terms of quality, quantity, speed, or
consistency?

Develop the time frame in which the work is to be accomplished.
Specify deadlines, time frames, due dates, and check
points for evaluating progress.

Once you go through the process, rethink it all to firm it up.
Check with team members who will be accountable for
accomplishing the work to verify that they understand exactly what
is expected and confirm "buy-in" on their part. Ask for more
feedback and then rewrite the goal if necessary.

Following are some sample S.M.A.R.T. goals/objectives:

- ❏ Design, develop, and implement a system for tracking
payments by February 10th. The tracking system should be
able to indicate the payment's date of receipt, its dollar
amount, and its date of deposit.
- ❏ Within the next 90 days, reduce the rejection rate for deluxe
whiz-bang widgets from the present level of eight percent to
a maximum of four percent.
- ❏ Produce a feasibility report for the director by April 15th
to determine whether the company can manufacture,
advertise, and distribute a new printer model for under

follow up

$250 a unit assuming a minimum annual sales volume of 100,000 units.

By making a commitment to develop a common purpose and set the ground rules for your team, you can ensure that expectations are aligned and you will have a unified front to successfully engage any challenges. People must clearly know the purpose, priorities (values and behavioral expectations), and strategic goals/objectives to create a vision for your team's success.

Practical Application

1. Write a purpose statement for your team. Remember to make it short enough for your team members to commit to memory. Next briefly describe what success should look like if you were to accomplish your purpose. This will become your vision statement.

2. Meet with your team members and draft four to six core value statements that reflect your core priorities. Discuss how each may be put into action to show that it really is a team value. You may want to rank your values in order to minimize any differences between the team's preferred values and its true values—the values actually reflected by members' behaviors. One way to do this is to record each preferred value on an index card and then ask each member to rank the values with "1," "2," or "3." in terms of the priority needed by the organization, with 3 indicating the value of highest importance to the team or organization and 1 being least important. Next go through the cards again to rank how each member thinks the values are actually being enacted with 3 indicating the values are fully enacted and 1 indicating the value is hardly reflected at all. Once you have performed this evaluation, address any discrepancies where a value is highly preferred (ranked with a 3), but hardly enacted (ranked with a 1).

3. Establish a set of ground rules by which team members will conduct business both internally and externally. These rules should be reflective of your values.

4. Develop some new S.M.A.R.T. goals/objectives for your team or go back and firm up old ones. Meet with team members to solicit feedback and discuss how each may be accomplished.

3.
Commit to Creating a Learning Environment

"An investment in knowledge
always pays the best interest."
—Benjamin Franklin

The U.S. Department of Labor recently published a report identifying the major strengths that American workers fundamentally lack. These include:

- ❑ skills in problem solving
- ❑ developing technical innovations
- ❑ interpersonal communication
- ❑ working with a team
- ❑ getting along with their boss

Another study by the American Society for Training and Development revealed that workers consistently see their managers and supervisors as confused about performance expectations, slow to respond to serious problems, and unable to articulate a clear vision for their groups.

The simple truth is new skills and new attitudes are currently needed at *every* organizational level. In order to build a high performance team you must create a learning environment. It is absolutely essential to increase knowledge at all levels if you want to successfully deal with the issues that are facing your team today and in the future.

It was Peter Senge's 1990 book *The Fifth Discipline* that popularized and brought the concept of the "learning organization" to the limelight. According to Senge, learning environments inspire people to continually expand their capacity to achieve the objectives they desire. New and expansive patterns of thinking are nurtured as people are set free to aspire and create. In a learning environment people see the whole picture together and are more flexible and adaptive to change. They are able to continually re-create themselves to soar higher.

Being a part of a high performance team gives people an opportunity to connect to something larger than themselves. The collective knowledge of the team produces a generative process for individuals to create greater and greater outcomes. As a wise person once observed, "None of us are as smart as *all* of us!"

Levels of Learning

Creating a learning environment is not about simply adding more training. While training is essential to develop certain types of skill, a learning environment involves the development of higher levels of knowledge in addition to skills. Learning takes place at the following four levels:

- ❑ **Processes**—Members must know and understand the team purpose, values and rules, and work objectives along with the skills needed to complete them. This may be accomplished through new member orientation and on-the-job training to provide the knowledge and facts needed to perform at expected standards.
- ❑ **New job skills**—New job skills are often required in situations where existing practices need to be changed or updated. This may require the help of outside expertise unless the knowledge is currently available inside the team. Learning new job skills can also be accomplished through

cross-training, which is one of the most effective ways to increase your knowledge base and create greater appreciation for what fellow team members do. Another method is called "shadowing" where a person follows or shadows another person to expand their awareness of what that person does. This is especially helpful across departmental lines to gain insight of the entire work process. It is also helpful for management personnel to shadow staff workers to get feedback on needed procedural changes or improvements.

 ❑ **Analytical thinking**—By learning to engage in analytical thinking, people learn to be adaptable to change and uncertainty. Not every problem will have a step-by-step process defined to address it. People must learn to respond to unexpected events in a productive way. This can only be accomplished by creating an environment where people are free to experiment and take risks—to see what works and what doesn't. Learning lessons from successes and failures of experimentation is the most effective way to sharpen critical thinking skills.

 ❑ **Self-mastery**—Teams learn through individuals who learn to be learners. Self-mastery is the discipline of continually seeking to deepen one's personal vision and to focus energies on designing the future rather than merely adapting to it. People with a high level of self-mastery live in a continual learning mode, never thinking of themselves as "arriving." It is a state where few things are thought of in terms of black and white. Self-mastery is not something to be possessed. Instead it is looked upon as a process, a lifelong discipline. People with a high level of self-mastery are acutely aware of their ignorance, their incompetence, and their own personal growth areas. Yet, they are deeply self-confident. Self-mastery sees the "journey as the reward."

Leading in the Learning Environment

Peter Senge argues that organizations which promote a learning environment require a new style of leadership, one that varies from the traditional style where the leader makes all the key decisions, sets the direction, and motivates the troops. The old style has a disempowering effect on people while the new style empowers individuals to become decision-makers and catalysts for positive change.

Senge refers to these new leaders as designers, stewards, and teachers. They are responsible for building an environment where people continue to expand their own ability to understand complexity and to clarify their role in fulfilling the team vision.

- **Designers**—The functions of designers are not easily observable, yet they have the most sweeping influence on the team or organization. The key areas of design are the purpose and core values by which team members should live. Building a shared purpose is crucial for long-term success and learning. In this function leaders are responsible for designing the learning processes that enable team members to deal productively with the critical issues and develop self-mastery. As a designer your role will be to create a work environment where people clearly understand the purpose, core values, and work standards. This is not a one-time event, but a continuous and repeated process of explaining and refining the rules.
- **Stewards**—These are the "holders" of the vision. It doesn't mean they own it. It is not their possession. Stewards see the vision as part of something larger than themselves. They choose service over self-interest, managing for the benefit of others. Their role is to tell the story that relates why the team has its purpose—a story that inspires others to live the vision. Stewards learn to listen to others' version of the vision and change their own when necessary. In this way they allow others to be involved in the re-creation and sharing of the team purpose.
- **Teachers**—This is not about "teaching" people how to achieve the team purpose. Instead, the role of the leader as teacher is to foster an environment of learning and to be committed to truth. Senge states that *the first responsibility*

of a leader is to define reality. While they may draw inspiration from their sense of stewardship, a teacher's real power lies in helping people achieve more accurate and more insightful views of reality. They lead people to see "the big picture" and to appreciate the cultural factors that determine the behaviors necessary to achieve the vision. Teachers create and manage creative tension, especially when a gap exists between vision and reality. They see the truth in changing situations and help facilitate a shift when necessary.

Utilize Action-Based Training

Industry studies conclude that organizations which provide regular training have higher employee retention, greater job satisfaction, and consequently more long-term success. The key is to provide quality training that has the greatest impact for the time invested.

The most effectual training methodology is behavior modeling. This action-based technique is highly effective in teaching people new interpersonal or technical skills, as well as the knowledge of why, when, and how to use the skills. When they return to the job, people experience heightened self-esteem and positive attitudes about their work because new skills bring increased recognition and satisfaction for a job well done.

The principles behind behavior modeling may best be described by the words of ancient Chinese philosopher Confucius, who wrote, *"I hear and I forget. I see and I remember. I do and I understand."* Following these principles, Hippocrates learned the art of healing, Churchill learned to orate, and Mozart learned to play the piano.

Behavior modeling can be a catalyst for wide-range team growth. This type of training facilitates behavioral change at every level of the organization by helping people improve how they work, how they feel about their work, and how they perceive leadership.

Behavior modeling offers a blueprint for accelerated learning. Students first observe the clear demonstration of a skill, then emulate and teach it to build competence and self-confidence. They are given the opportunity to practice new skills and to plan their own practical application in a safe environment with constructive, performance-enhancing feedback. A typical behavior-modeling training program would include the following steps:

1. Describe the performance areas of a skill and why they are important.
2. Solicit feedback from participants on how the training might be enhanced or customized to more suitably meet their needs and requirements.
3. Demonstrate the skill components in a manner that is effective for a wide range of learning styles, including audio, visual, and kinesthetic (hands-on).
4. Set up training opportunities for participants to practice the skill repeatedly with constructive feedback.
5. Allow participants to reflect on specific practical applications of the skill.
6. Express confidence and support.
7. Provide a summary of the items covered and arrange a follow-up date for ongoing feedback and performance evaluation.
8. Set up teach-back opportunities where the person teaches others what they have learned to reinforce learning. The most effective way to get people to learn is to have them teach others.

To reiterate the importance of step number eight above: A manager related to me how he sent one of his supervisors to a training class and asked her to put together a presentation to give to the other staff members about what she learned at the class. The supervisor spent hours putting it all together and her manager remarked, "She learned more from giving her presentation than she did from the original training." When you send people for training have them come back and teach others.

Characteristics of a Learning Environment

Here are some characteristics of a learning environment:

❏ **Focus is on the future**—These teams have their eyes fixed on the future. They continually scan the landscape, preparing for upcoming changes and challenges by developing the skills and resources needed to fulfill the vision and purpose.

❏ **Information flows in all directions**—Processes are set in place to ensure that expertise is available where it is needed. It may come from internal or external sources. Individuals are encouraged to network across organizational boundaries to develop their own knowledge and proficiency. The free flow of information also reduces incidents of group stagnation as ideas remain fresh and innovative.

❏ **Leaders are committed to people development**—Learning is rewarded. Leaders support training and people at all levels are provided opportunities for personal and professional development. People are given the time and resources for exploring, reflecting, understanding, and developing their thinking power.

❏ **People are valued**—Individual ideas and creativity are stimulated by an environment of openness and trust. Those ideas are actually used and people are acknowledged and often rewarded for them. Diversity is viewed and celebrated as a strength. People are encouraged to speak out and views can be challenged from all directions without fear of repercussion.

❏ **Learning takes place from experience**—Learning from mistakes often has a greater impact than learning from success. In the learning environment failure is not only tolerated, it is encouraged provided the lessons are learned. This promotes a "play-to-win" mentality rather than playing not to lose.

Teams that nurture a learning environment have many advantages. People have more fun which creates a higher amount of enthusiasm and productivity. People are more optimistic about the future. Creativity flourishes. It is safe to take risks with new ideas and behaviors that help people stretch beyond their perceived limits. Everyone's opinions are valued regardless of their position.

A New Age in Business

We are currently witnessing one of the most significant changes in the history of work as we move out of the Industrial Age into the Information Age. These have also been referred to as the Manual Workers Age and the Knowledge Workers Age, respectively. Productivity has risen fifty-fold as the emphasis shifts from equipment to people as our greatest capital.

In his book *Management Challenges of the 21st Century*, Peter Drucker describes it this way:

> "The most important, and indeed the truly unique, contribution of management in the 20th century was the fifty-fold increase in productivity of the Manual Worker in manufacturing. The most important contribution management needs to make in the 21st century is similarly to increase the productivity of Knowledge Work and the Knowledge Worker. The most valuable assets of a 20th-century company were its production equipment. The most valuable asset of a 21st-century institution, whether business or non-business, will be its knowledge workers and their productivity."

The way of thinking that produced the success of the Industrial Age still dominates much of the workplace today, but it simply will not work in the new Information/Knowledge Worker age. Einstein said, *"The significant problems we face cannot be solved at the same level of thinking we were at when we created them."* If you are to succeed in the new century, you must create a learning environment.

Practical Application

1. How is your team preparing for the future? What changes or challenges loom on the horizon and what new skills will your team members need?

2. What processes do you have set up by which people can exchange information or cross-train? How are you soliciting feedback from outside sources to gain fresh, new perspectives?

3. How are you encouraging and providing personal development opportunities for your team? Is the training dollar the last item budgeted for and the first thing cut during austere times? Do you have a tuition assistance program in place to provide opportunities for employees to continue their education at the local college or vocational school?

4. How do you show people that they are valued? Do you listen to their ideas and use them? What are the ways diversity strengthens your team?

5. What do you do to encourage risk-taking? How do you ensure that people "fail forward" by learning from their mistakes? Would you say that your team is playing to win or playing not to lose?

How do I get them to buy in on credit + Mentor there

Involve the team
w/ Bonus potential

4.

Commit to Sharing the Profits and Losses

*"Any business arrangement that is not profitable to the
other person will in the end prove unprofitable for you.
That bargain that yields mutual satisfaction is the only one
that is apt to be repeated."*
—B. C. Forbes

I recently spoke at a company staff meeting where people were really excited to be there. I asked what all the enthusiasm was about and they informed me that they had just received their quarterly profit-sharing checks. One woman, a clerical worker, ecstatically told me, "They started profit-sharing here a little over four years ago and my first check was two hundred dollars. Today I received a check for *four thousand dollars!*" she said. Wow, was she happy to be on the team. In fact, everyone in the room was happy to be there.

I frequently provide training for another organization that is in the same industry as the company above. Instead of sharing profits like the company above, this one offers a quarterly bonus incentive in the form of a trip to all its employees. If they hit a specified sales goal, the company springs for a trip somewhere of the owners' choosing. If an employee chooses not to take the trip, then it's his or her tough luck—no bonus!

In the first situation people are absolutely thrilled to be a part of the team. In the second people grumble, especially those with children or other family situations that make taking a company trip unattractive or prohibitive. One of their employees commented to me, "They think that we're supposed to be excited about their stupid trips. I can't afford to take my children on these trips and I don't want to spend that time away from my family. And to add insult to injury they make us take vacation days if we go—and they call this an incentive bonus? If I choose not to take the trip I get nothing—that's their rule," she bemoaned. "This is very de-motivating."

Which of these two practices do you think has the greatest positive impact on their teams? The answer is fairly obvious. The first company is on target to exceed their yearly sales goals and have realized an annual growth in excess of twenty percent. Their employee retention rate is excellent and the staff is optimistic and enthused about being with the company.

On the other hand, the second company missed their yearly sales goal by over forty percent and experienced negative annual growth. In other words, they are moving backwards. Employee turnover rate is high. They have lost many key people in the past year and will probably lose more because of morale issues.

The bottom line is: Sharing the profits will definitely boost the morale and performance of your team, as long as it is something that people value.

Co-Create Your Success

This whole notion of sharing the profits of business took roots in 1842 with a bright idea by a French house-painter named Edme-Jean Leclaire, who is commonly referred to today as the Father of Profit-Sharing. He thought, "If I give back a portion of the profits to the workmen, I bet they'd work smarter and we could turn even more profit." His motivation wasn't to get them to work harder because they already worked hard as it was. If he could get them to become more efficient at their work, they could save a substantial amount of money each year for the business and he could pass on the profits. This arrangement proved to be a great success—the efficiency *and* morale of the men increased remarkably as did their material gain. This also proved to be a great success for Leclaire, who began life with nothing and died a wealthy man. He always maintained that without the enthusiasm and commitment drawn out in his men by profit-sharing, he would never have grown such a large business or gained so much wealth. They became co-creators in one another's success.

Leclaire's system aroused the interest of John Stuart Mill and other economists in the 1860s and profit-sharing began to be experimented with throughout the Western industrialized world. There have been many successes and failures in the course of this experimentation. The successes seem to have a common theme: *Someone breathed a spirit of partnership into the plan.* And often it has led to actual partnership where workers not only received a share of profits, but also an opportunity to invest in the ownership of the business.

As a partner or shareholder of the business, the workers take their share of the profits paid on capital, as well as responsibility for losses, if any. In this type of agreement workers have a certain amount of control or ownership of the business. What better environment could you ask for when workers walk through the door each morning and proclaim, "I own this place."

Profit-Sharing is a term frequently used to describe other forms of additions to ordinary wages, such as bonuses on output or quality of work. Yet, many of these are not actually profit-sharing. If your team members are awarded a specified amount of money or prizes if sales meet or exceed a certain quantity, or the quality exceeds a certain standard, technically that is called gain-sharing. Even when the bonus depends strictly on profit, it is not actually profit-sharing if it is confined to the employees who are highest ranking or top performing.

It is not really profit-sharing either, when an employer or boss takes something from his profits at his own will and pleasure, and gives it to his employees. Cash gifts are considered to be gratuities. When gifts take other forms, such as better offices, memberships to the local health club, recreation rooms, or provisions for sickness or retirement, all given at the will of the owner, they are known as paternalism. On the surface these practices might appear to be okay, but be beware—gratuities and paternalism are not partnership. Partnership results in co-ownership while the other two lead to an environment where workers look at the owner or boss as the parent figure. And when workers look at the boss as a parent what do they often act like? Children!

If you are currently awarding bonuses or awards to the highest performers on your team, be careful not to create a competitive environment that is counterproductive. I have seen countless organizations in which a "me" versus "we" mentality exists because of competition over team members chasing the same few bonus dollars. This may destroy the cohesiveness and long-term success of a team.

Rank Doesn't Have Privilege   *Everyone works the same*

Although profit-sharing has been proven to be effective in increasing productivity and profits, it is either grossly underused or poorly administered by organizations today. I am amazed at how many small business owners have admitted to me that the thought of profit-sharing had not even entered their mind until I brought it up. These are also the type of leaders who complain because people don't care about the job. When asked, "How many people do you have working for you?" they respond, "About half."

Many companies have profit-sharing but it is reserved only for their management team, the chosen few. There is a danger when companies grant only management personnel the favor of receiving profit-sharing and other special benefits. This generates a mentality that rank has privilege, and I'm sorry, but that's just plain wrong.

A friend related the following story: He was traveling across country and one of his connecting flights had been canceled because of bad weather. He was standing in the customer service line to try and arrange booking on a later flight. Several flights had been canceled so the line was rather long. He had finally made his way to the counter, after almost an hour wait, when a man stepped up to the head of the line and tried to cut in front of the others who had been waiting. Apparently this man was an executive for that particular airline company and had also been booked on one of the canceled flights.

The young woman at the service counter politely told the man that he would have to step to the back of the line and wait his turn like everyone else. The man became indignant that she would put him, a company executive for god's-sake, to such inconvenience! "Do you know who I am?" he demanded. Without any hesitation the young woman at the counter replied, "Hold on one second, Sir," then immediately announced on the loudspeaker, "Attention, ladies and gentleman, we have a man at the counter who doesn't know who he is. If anyone recognizes him, would you please come forward?"

The man walked away embarrassed as the people in line applauded the young woman at the counter to show their approval of how she courageously and rather humorously handled this bully. You see, this man was under the mistaken impression that rank has privilege.

Rank does not have privilege, it has responsibility. If you want to build a high performance team, you must know this and practice it. If you want people to partner with you in the success of your organization, you must treat them as partners, rather than subordinates. This requires a spirit of humility, which is the cornerstone of great leadership.

Choose a Plan

Any proposed profit-sharing plan should be approved in advance by the Internal Revenue Service. There are two common types of plans: the cash plan and the deferred plan. Some organizations choose both which is called "combination" profit-sharing.

Under the cash plan, profits are distributed in cash—usually quarterly, semiannually, or annually. Total profit to be paid to the employees is usually an amount fixed by a formula. For example, one company's employees receive thirty percent of net profits before taxes, but not to exceed twenty percent of the payroll.

Under the deferred plan, a trust fund is set up to provide employees with future benefits. The fund is created by contributions from both participating employees and the company, according to a formula. The deferred plan may provide health and life insurance, retirement accounts, disability payments, and supplemental unemployment benefits. Additionally, some deferred plans provide for loan privileges and cash withdrawals, which provide immediate financial assistance in time of need.

In addition, employers may set up 401(k) benefits plans in which they contribute to individuals' accounts. Most employers match individual 401(k) contributions which gives individuals an immediate return on their investment. Many profit-sharing/401(k) plans permit participants to purchase their employer's stock which also encourages employee ownership.

Profit-sharing plans have three major benefits:

❏ They become a unifying force that unites management and non-management employees.
❏ They provide a definite work incentive because employees can see that the profitability of the business and their personal welfare are essentially related.
❏ Each worker is enticed to be more creative in increasing sales and reducing or eliminating expenses.

For advice or examples on profit-sharing plans contact:

Council of Profit-Sharing Industries
20 North Wacker Dr., Suite 3700
Chicago, Illinois 60606
www.psca.org

Create smart plans where needed

Share the Losses

I believe that it is equally important to share losses when they occur. People take ownership of the team or organization when they share both profits *and* losses. When your team reaps the rewards and assumes the risks of doing business they will make a physical, emotional, and mental investment in quality performance.

Many organizations are quick to jump on the sharing-the-losses wagon. They down-size, cut benefits, reduce pay, or whatever it takes to "stop the bleeding" and understandably so. I see no problem with this practice as long as it is administered fairly across the board.

Unfortunately, many organizations do not share losses equally. Often the workforce is downsized and benefits are cut, while at the same time executives vote themselves exorbitant raises or bonuses.

In a highly publicized case recently, a national airline company appeared to be headed toward bankruptcy. Upper management was trying to cut costs in various areas. They had been negotiating with the labor union for the airplane mechanics to reduce their pay. The union balked at the proposal and I don't blame them. You see, at the same time the executives of this company were negotiating cuts in pay for their employees, it came to light that they had voted themselves generous bonuses for the year. Hello? What's wrong with this picture? What were these people thinking? And what is the cost of doing business this way? Plenty in terms of morale, trust, and productivity.

Similarly, I know a city manager who accepted a fifteen percent raise in salary, while at the same time proposed to lay off several firefighters because of budgetary constraints. This is no way to win friends and influence people. If you are going to ask people to sacrifice, you must lead by example and make an equal or greater sacrifice yourself, and at the very least don't take a raise while cutting others' pay.

The Southwest Way

Let me tell you about an organization who is doing it right in this area. In fact, Southwest Airlines has been doing lots of things right for a long time. They have turned consistent profits for over 25 years, while most of the other large carriers have gone bankrupt or struggled. They also have one of the most team-oriented cultures I have seen.

I was invited last year to speak to a group of their leaders. In the course of the meeting I heard them recount how the company had taken a major financial hit after the terrorist attacks in New York City on September 11th, 2001. For the first time in 25 years they were facing serious cutbacks. After much deliberation, the management team overwhelmingly resolved that they would not cut people. After all, people have been their greatest asset and the primary reason they have been successful for so many years. They would find other ways to reduce costs.

It was particularly inspiring to hear Colleen Barrett, the company president, recall how, in the face of austerity, she received personal checks and letters from SWA employees—from mechanics and flight attendants, to reservation clerks and pilots—pledging to donate a portion of their earnings or vacation pay to help pull the company through that tough time.

As a leader, let me ask, "When was the last time your employees offered to give *you* a check?" Loyalty, sacrifice, and sustaining success are all fruits of partnership in sharing both profits and losses.

Make People Feel Important

Many years ago, when my son was a young boy, we regularly took walks together in the woods. Being a typically rambunctious boy, he never walked beside me. Rather, he would constantly run ahead, then stop and wait for me to catch up. One day while on one of our walks, he ran ahead of me then crawled up on a big rock and sat down to rest. When I caught up with him, he said, "Daddy, let's just sit on this rock and talk for a while." I climbed up on the rock, sat beside him, and said, "Okay. What do you want to talk about?" He responded with utmost seriousness, "I don't care, just as long as it's *important!*"

So it is with each member of your team. We all have an innate need to feel important to those around us. People want to count for something. You may not be in a situation where you can share monetary wealth, but you will garner a great amount of dedication and effort by acknowledging and validating people. When you make people feel as though who they are and what they have to say is important, they will give every ounce of strength to perform what you request. As a famous field general once observed, "Men will die for ribbons."

One of the most effective ways to make others feel important is to genuinely listen to them. Actively and intently engage them by giving full attention to what they have to say. Another way to acknowledge people is to solicit their input and feedback about upcoming decisions that affect them and the team. By including people in the decision-making process, they will take a greater amount of ownership for their personal contribution to the success of the team.

Practical Application

1. Do you currently have a profit-sharing plan in place? If not, why? Contact the Council for Profit-Sharing to get information.

2. If you currently have a bonus or incentive program, how is it working? Is it limited to certain staff members? Does it motivate people to take ownership in the business or is it de-motivating? Ask your staff. If you are currently awarding prizes, such as trips, think about the practicality. Often these become a source of stress, rather than pleasure or reward.

3. Have you solicited feedback from your staff about how they would like to be remunerated for high performance? One of the best ways to do this is through an employee survey. I have found through discussions with thousands of people that there are two common things that you can't go wrong with in rewarding people—*giving money or time off with pay.*

4. Do you send out a message that "rank has privilege" by giving extra bonuses or benefits to management? If so, beware—this may quench the spirit of partnership in your organization.

5. How do you share losses when they occur? Leaders should lead by example when sacrifices are required.

5.

Be honest

Commit to Turning Around Poor Performance

*"Leadership is lifting a person's vision to higher sights,
the raising of a person's performance to a higher standard."*
—Peter F. Drucker

On many occasions throughout my years of leadership training and performance coaching, I have listened to managers describe the anguish of confronting employees about poor performance. What I often hear are rationalizations for their own reluctance to deal with these awkward and challenging issues in an effective manner.

When a person's poor performance does not change it creates problems for you, your team, and your organization. You must turn it around, but keep in mind: <u>Your goal in correcting performance problems should be to positively influence future behavior and to build motivation for continued improvement for both the individual and the team.</u>

Clarify Performance Expectations

A young man went to the pet store in search of a singing canary. He was a bachelor and it seemed that his house was too quiet, so he thought that he would buy a bird to liven things up a bit. The store owner had just the bird for him, so the man bought it.

The next day the man came home from work to a house filled with music. He went to the cage to feed his bird and noticed for the first time that the canary had only one leg. He felt cheated. He could not believe that he had been sold a one-legged bird!

He called the pet store owner and complained. "What do you want," responded the owner, "a canary that can sing or one that can dance?"

When you don't make it clear to people about what you need or want, the stage will be set for failed expectations like the man above experienced. This often leads to wasted time and resources, in addition to frustration, disappointment, and conflict.

You must establish and clarify performance expectations as early as possible in a working relationship. This involves having *regular*, mutual discussions to create a shared understanding of responsibilities, priorities, measurable goals, and a performance-tracking plan. It is a good idea to discuss expectations when:

- ❏ The person is new to the team, job assignment, or task.
- ❏ The team is changing directions or needs to realign efforts to meet new goals.
- ❏ The person has asked for clarification about priorities and/or goals.
- ❏ A new performance phase is beginning.
- ❏ The person is struggling or not meeting current expectations.

Although you may be clear about what the team is trying to achieve, the other person may not be. If necessary, describe the relationship between their performance and the goals of their team members. This will help them to see how their work contributes to the big picture. It may be helpful to draw a simple diagram to show the relationship between individual member's functions.

It is important to discuss responsibilities and priorities with every team member. Jointly determine the extent to which each individual task contributes to the team goals, and mutually establish a list of priorities that balances team effectiveness with competing personal demands. The key here is to *jointly determine* and *mutually establish* these expectations. If this process is interactive, the chance of buy-in will be greatly increased. People are much more motivated to accomplish goals that they help define.

Another vital step in the process of establishing performance expectations will be to mutually determine how goals will be measured and tracked. Make sure that every team member understands exactly what is being measured and how it is being measured, so each may individually assess how they are doing on meeting expectations. There should be no surprises when it comes to performance evaluation. The key is to keep communication flowing in both directions to catch misunderstandings or misalignments as early as possible.

Harness the Pygmalion and Galatea Effects

Your expectations of people and their expectations of themselves are key factors in how well people perform their jobs. The Pygmalion effect, often known as the power of expectations, deduces that people perform in ways that are consistent with the expectations they have picked up from their leader both consciously and unconsciously.

In a classic Pygmalion study, schoolteachers were led to believe that some of their students possessed exceptionally high potential while others did not. Unknown to the teachers, however, the fact is the so-called high-potential students were selected at random. In actuality, all students were equal in potential and were merely "labeled" as high, regular, or low potential. Interestingly, as the experiment unfolded, differences began to emerge, not on the basis of any innate intelligence or other predisposed factors, but solely on the basis of the expectancy of the teachers. Over time, the students with high teacher expectations began to significantly overshadow all others in actual achievement.

If a leader has high expectations of his or her subordinates, their self-confidence and productivity will grow. Performance improves when supervisors communicate positive thoughts to people about

set high goals for all

themselves. If a supervisor truly believes that an employee has the ability to make a positive contribution at work, the conveyance of that message, either consciously or unconsciously, will positively affect that person's performance. Furthermore, when a supervisor holds positive expectations about an individual, he or she actually helps the person boost their own self-concept and self-esteem. And when people believe they can succeed and make a positive contribution to the team, their performance rises to the level of their own expectations.

The Galatea effect is even more powerful than the Pygmalion effect in improving employee performance. Sometimes referred to as "self-fulfilling prophecy," the Galatea effect can be interpreted to mean that an individual's opinion about his ability and his self-expectations about his performance will largely determine how well he will perform. In other words, if a person thinks he can succeed, he will likely succeed.

A frog and scorpion were sitting beside a river one day. The scorpion asked if he could catch a ride on the frog's back across to the other side. The frog said, "Uh, I don't think so." The scorpion asked why and the frog responded, "Because you're a scorpion and scorpions sting frogs. If you sting me I'll die!" The scorpion said, "Don't be ridiculous, mister frog, if I stung you then I would die, too!"

The frog thought about it and said, "Okay, that makes sense. Hop on." Halfway across the river, what happens? The scorpion stings the frog! The frog is incredulous. On his third time going down he said, "I can't believe it! You stung me, but now you're going to die, too. Why?" The scorpion shrugged and replied, "Because I'm a scorpion, and that's what scorpions do. They sting frogs!"

As absurd as this story sounds, it characterizes human behavior. People will do anything they can to make their actions congruent with what they think or believe about themselves, regardless of how destructive or tragic it may turn out to be. *If you want people to change behavior, you must change their thoughts and beliefs.*

A leader who can assist individuals to believe in themselves and in their worth, has harnessed a powerful performance improvement tool. Here are actions you can take to encourage and build positive, powerful self-expectations in the workplace:

❑ Provide opportunities for the individual to experience increasingly challenging work assignments and allow them adequate time to succeed before moving to the next level.

❑ Provide developmental opportunities that reflect what the individual is interested in learning.

❑ Give frequent, positive feedback to consistently communicate your confidence in their ability to perform the job.

❑ Provide one-to-one coaching with an emphasis on improving what the individual does well rather than focusing on their weaknesses.

❑ Assign a senior colleague or team leader to serve in a mentoring role with the individual.

❑ Project a genuine commitment to their success and ongoing development.

Don't Mistake Potential for Skill

Todd was bright, enthusiastic, and responsible. Although he had no experience, I hired him to manage a retail business, based on his great potential. From the beginning, I told him that I had confidence in his ability and offered full support for the decisions he made about the daily operations. But I remained a hands-off manager, offering little or no direction as to how that would be done.

Within a short time I noticed that his enthusiasm began to wane—and so did the profits. I stopped by occasionally and gave him a pep talk, assuring him he had my full support. But this had little effect, as the business continued to spiral downward. Soon he began to avoid making eye contact with me when I came into the store and I began to second-guess my decision to hire him. Maybe he couldn't handle the responsibility after all, I thought.

After a little less than a year, we both became highly dissatisfied. He wasn't happy with the job and I wasn't happy with the way he was performing. I thought, "He is bankrupting my

Know when to let go of people

business!" We finally reached a mutual decision to part ways. He left the business with a bad taste in his mouth.

In retrospect, I don't blame him. Who was really bankrupting my business? I take responsibility for this misfortunate situation. I set Todd up for failure from the beginning by not giving him the direction he needed to manage the business. When I looked at him, all I saw was his potential, thinking, "If I can just keep him motivated, he will be successful."

If you want people to perform at their highest level, you must adapt your leadership style to their *current* developmental needs. Do not mistake potential, intelligence, or past successes for skill. If a person does not have the knowledge or the experience to perform the task, all the supportive words in the world will not make them successful. They must be adequately trained in order to gain the know-how to do the job.

First, look at the situation and assess the developmental needs of the person. Consider the following checkpoints:

❑ Identify the specific task that is required and the knowledge needed to accomplish it.

❑ Determine the individual's current skill level. Can he or she perform the task to the desired standard? If not, do they have transferable skills upon which to build new competencies quickly? If the individual possesses low levels of task skill, give direction by teaching them how to do the task (see Chapter 3 on experience-based learning), establishing work objectives and expectations, and closely monitoring and evaluating their performance.

❑ Are they motivated? Are they confident? If they are low in these areas provide support by: soliciting two-way communication and feedback; providing encouragement; involving them in the decision-making process; promoting self-leadership.

Having The "Come to Jesus" Talk

Regardless of how hard you work to nurture growth and establish mutual understanding of what is expected, some people,

Be honest

for various reasons, simply won't perform or will do just barely enough to get by on the job. In those situations it is necessary to have that "come to Jesus" talk in which you will attempt to help the person to: (1) recognize the need for a change in behavior, and; (2) commit to turn their performance around.

Before engaging in that discussion, prepare a plan of action and then work your plan:

- ❏ **Do your homework**—Research and clarify the nature of the problem and the negative impact on people and productivity. Stick to the facts and be specific. Think about how the person might react when you bring up the issue and plan for ways to counter objections or excuses. If you are in doubt about legal issues consult with the Human Resources department first.

- ❏ **Clarify your objective**—Be clear on what you are trying to achieve and what the best outcome should be. Keep in mind, your goal in correcting performance problems should be to positively influence future behavior and to build motivation for continued improvement.

- ❏ **Talk with the person as soon as possible**—Start with a brief statement about the performance problem without being accusatory. A good opening statement sounds like, "The issue is progress on the project." By pinpointing the issue at the start, you will be able to keep the discussion focused and productive. Remain calm and be mindful of your tone of voice and body language. Confront with your words, but don't batter the person with a harsh tone or overbearing body gestures like pointing your finger in their face. *Be firm, but be nice.*

- ❏ **Jointly assess the issue**—Ask the person to express his or her understanding of the problem. In some cases, they may provide new information that might change your perception of the situation. By listening to their side of the story, you will help to build collaboration and reduce defensiveness, as you begin to develop a common picture of what is happening. Identify and come to terms with areas of

Don't pro-crastinate

disagreement. In some cases, you may need to gather additional information to get a clearer picture. Review and summarize the situation in light of what you have learned from this discussion.

❏ **Develop a mutual plan of action**—Mutually identify possible actions to improve the situation. By asking the person for input on identifying action steps you will encourage them to take ownership of the plan. Once you decide a plan of action, discuss how it will be measured, how often you will follow up, and possible consequences that may be incurred. Inform the person of any formal disciplinary actions you may take and let them know that you are available to clarify issues as they arise.

❏ **Ask for commitment**—Do not hesitate to ask for a commitment that going forward the person will perform the task exactly as expected. Studies show that over 90% of people comply when asked for a verbal or written commitment. Harness the principle of reciprocity to increase the chances of compliance even greater by committing something to them in return. *The best way to get someone to do something for you is to do something for them.*

Correcting Bad Attitudes

Attitude problems may be evidenced by an entitlement mentality with signs of rolling eyeballs, sighs, antagonistic body language, and other gestures or sometimes childish actions that can drive a manager crazy. The problem with this type of behavior is that it is so easily denied by those who do it. Additionally, the person doing it may be a high performer in that they meet all their measurable goals, but their attitude has a negative effect on the team performance. If a person performs well individually, but drags the team down, you must take action.

When attempting to eradicate this type of behavior tell the person how you perceive their actions and how you or others feel about it. If formal written discipline becomes necessary, very specifically cite the person's attitudinal actions and how they affect their work performance or that of their team. Avoid using the word "attitude" because it is too subjective. Cite specific behaviors and actions only.

In order to provide all the elements of workplace due process, here are some basic rules for administering progressive discipline:

☑ The employee should know specifically what the problem is and what action he or she needs to take to correct the problem.

❏ The employee should be given a reasonable and clearly stated time period in which to correct the problem.

❏ The employee should understand clearly the consequences for their lack of appropriate action to correct the problem.

❏ Be consistent in the application of your rules, according to written policies and past practices in handling similar types of offenses.

❏ Discipline should be appropriate for the seriousness of the offense. Your policy and procedures manual should help serve as a guideline.

❏ Employees should be allowed an opportunity to respond and provide input on their suggestions for a performance improvement plan.

You as a manager are responsible for fifty percent of the equation for performance issues. You must be distinctly clear and specific about what you expect and consistently provide adequate skills training, in addition to continuous feedback and the resources people need to do their job. <u>When people know exactly what is expected, they have a choice: they can either do the work as required, or not. Either way, there is a consequence for their decision.</u>

Practical Application

1. Do you currently have performance problems to correct? What are the facts surrounding the issue? Do you have first-hand knowledge of the situation? Beware of perceptions or hearsay of others.

2. Have you analyzed the person's current developmental status? Do they have the skills required to do the job? If not, they need more training.
3. Is the performance problem related to personality issues with co-workers? If so, you may consider reassignment, transfer, or coaching to help others recognize and appreciate differences in personal styles.
4. Have you fully explained job responsibilities and expectations? Does the person fully understand the importance of those responsibilities to the success of the team? Do they understand that what they do reflects back on the team? Have you conveyed confidence in their ability to do the job? Remember to harness the power of the Pygmalion and Galatea effects to help people believe that they can succeed in doing an outstanding job.
5. If the performance problem is caused by lack of commitment or attitudinal behavior you must take corrective action, which may possibly include termination. Poor performers and people with negative attitudes can become like a cancer, that over time, will threaten the long-term survival of the entire team.

Don't let poor performance affect others.

6.

we're loyal to

Commit to Dancing With "Those Who Brought You"

*"An ounce of loyalty is
worth a pound of cleverness."
—Elbert Hubbard*

A woman who works for a major corporation that just let thousands of people go in a major downsizing, told me: "This has been a terrible experience—so many people that I've known and worked with for years were demoted, booted out, or transferred. It has been difficult for everyone here. I still have my job, but I'll never feel the same about this company."

"I've been here over twenty years," she said, "and over that time we were given the sense that as long as we did a good job, the company would stand by us. Then all of a sudden we were told, 'No one is guaranteed a job anymore.'"

There is a growing unease that no one's job is safe anymore, even in a thriving economy. A major telecommunications company announced its intention to lay off forty thousand workers the same year it reported a record $5 billion profit. National recruiting firms report that more than half of callers making inquiries about jobs are still employed—but are fearful of losing their jobs. And a recent poll reported that one-third of Americans fear that someone in their household will lose their job.

One worker commented, "There's no way to give your loyalty to a company anymore and expect it to be returned. You're expected to be part of a team, yet be ready to move on upon short notice. So each person is becoming their own shop within the company."

Regardless of the services or products your team produces, people are your greatest asset. Of course you don't owe people a career or a living, but keep in mind that re-engineering or streamlining the organization is about more than reducing head counts and throwing people out of work. Loyalty runs two ways. If you want people to be loyal to the team, then they must perceive loyalty in return.

Continually invest in people by providing training to sharpen technical, problem-solving, and interpersonal skills to increase their value to both the team and their own marketability. Sure, some may gain new skills and leave for bigger opportunities. One manager complained to me about the cost of training people when many of them end up leaving for better jobs. I told him that it beat the alternative of *not training people and having them stay*.

The "Franchise" Player vs. "Team" Player

Sports franchises are notorious for blowing the salary cap on that one super star whom they hope will catapult the team to a championship. One such player reputedly stood in front of his new NFL teammates and rather brazenly introduced himself as "the reason the rest of you guys didn't get a raise this year." No doubt, this young man was a legend in his own mind, but his performance on the field never lived up to the billing. So-called franchise players rarely do.

Michael Jordan probably epitomizes the term as much as anyone in sports history. He is arguably the best basketball player to have ever stepped on the court, but he never wore a championship ring until Coach Phil Jackson came along and inspired him to put his efforts into helping those around him play well. Once Jordan made the transition from "franchise" player to "team" player, the Chicago Bulls won the next six out of seven NBA Championships.

I am not saying that you shouldn't recruit outstanding performers. I think it is smart to go after the best people you can get. But what message does it send when you blow the payroll on a hired gun, a mercenary who has no allegiance to anyone, while short sheeting their teammates who have been long devoted to the team? These situations seldom produce championship teams because of resentments that arise. Furthermore, many teams actually improve when the designated franchise player is lured away by a higher bidder. The highest performing and certainly the most fun teams to be associated with are comprised of "no-name" players who don't have their egos tied to who gets top billing.

It is refreshing to see people who are truly "team-players" in today's world. I recently read a story about a coach who is so widely known for his loyalty to his team that one sportswriter described him this way: *"He not only dances with those who brought him, he doesn't even know anyone else is at the sock hop!"*

Establish Mentoring Programs   *Have the good ones help out*

One of the best ways to dance with those who brought you is to promote people from within your organization. In order to promote from within effectively, establish a formal mentoring program to teach the skill sets needed for team members to move to the next level.

The concept of mentoring has been around over three thousand years, since Odysseus, the hero of Homer's Odyssey, entrusted the education of his son to an advisor and friend named Mentor. Although the term is rooted in mythology, it has grown throughout the history to be one of the most effective tools for human development.

In establishing a mentorship program the first thing you will need to do is select qualified individuals to serve as mentors. They should be senior colleagues or team leaders who possess expertise

Partner for success

in organizational functions, a commitment to the program, and the time to provide tutelage to apprentices. It is also important for mentors to be *people-oriented, flexible, dependable, and collaborative, with a willingness to nurture and help others.*

Successful mentoring skills can be taught through train-the-trainer courses that focus on communication and active listening techniques, effective teaching methods, situational leadership and coaching models, conflict resolution, and problem-solving skills.

The relationship between the mentor and apprentice is highly important to the success of the program. It is essential that both parties trust one another and have a genuine desire to undertake the mentoring relationship. They should also work in close enough proximity to make it feasible. Various factors may be considered to increase trust, such as pairing people of same gender, compatible personality types, or common cultural background, but are not always necessary.

A mentor's role is synonymous with teacher, coach, trainer, role model, counselor, and leader. He or she may assist in the development of professional and/or personal goals in an ongoing, supportive relationship. Specific goals and expectations should be clarified regarding the process and the extent of the relationship. Without them, a formal mentoring program is destined for failure. If you don't know your destination, how will you know when you have arrived?

After goals and expectations are clarified for the mentoring relationship, the next step is to decide the right tasks to share and the logistics for conducting formal and informal one-on-one and group meetings. Make sure that the physical setting is conducive to learning—quiet enough to discuss training points, yet not too isolated where people feel disconnected from the rest of the team— and schedule enough time to adequately cover the subject matter and answer questions.

A system of monitoring and supporting mentors should also be established in the program to provide opportunities for guidance and program assessment. Checkpoints, in the form of meetings, phone calls, or e-mail, should be scheduled periodically to keep the lines of communication open with mentors.

An effective mentoring program will benefit the team by:

❑ Enhancing personal work ethics.
❑ Elevating work standards.
❑ Developing greater interests in individual tasks.
❑ Increasing creative expression of individual talents.
❑ Enlarging the knowledge base.
❑ Establishing a "line of sight" to the team vision and mission.

Utilize Reverse Mentoring

In his book, *Leading Up: How to Lead Your Boss So You Both Win*, Wharton management professor Michael Useem described how General Electric, under the leadership of former CEO Jack Welch, made massive strides in embracing the concept of "reverse mentoring." At GE everyone is expected to challenge his or her leaders, even if it meant challenging Welch himself.

GE already had a well-established mentoring program in place, where all senior management members were given the charge to mentor the next generation of the company's top talent, when Welch observed, "E-business knowledge is generally inversely proportional to both age and height in the organization." To counter balance this phenomenon, the company launched a "reverse mentoring" program in which 600 worldwide executives were asked to reach down into the ranks and pick younger people to mentor them on the intricacies of the Internet and Web development. Welch set the example by choosing his own mentor who ran GE's main Website.

The mentoring program did more than give executives Web site and E-business orientations. It opened the lines of communication for leadership to flow both upward and downward much easier within the organization. The mid-level managers felt more comfortable in feeding ideas to their bosses and pressing change at the top. And top-level managers experienced a greater sense of ease in eliciting insights from below. The entire organization benefited from the process.

When people are granted the responsibility to "lead upward," leaders not only encourage it, they fully expect to have their

Start utilizing their skills.

decisions challenged by team members who are often closer to customers and more familiar with the products of the business. This practice will help to avoid falling into the trap of groupthink—a situation where a few myopic leaders are calling all the shots. The Challenger space shuttle explosion was a prime example of what happens when leaders fall into this trap of not allowing others to challenge their decisions.

Let Others Drive the Bus

In their book *The Flight of the Buffalo* authors James Belasco and Ralph Stayer discuss the need for a change in the traditional leadership paradigm. They analogized the old leadership style as resembling a herd of buffaloes, where the leader is compared to the head buffalo, usually the most dominant bull, and the followers are like the herd. In comparison, the followers, like the buffalo herd, will not act independently without the guidance of the leader. The followers will stand immobilized and be slaughtered if the head buffalo is killed first.

In the old paradigm, leaders act like head buffaloes, giving orders and making solitary decisions. Everyone else is a member of the herd, relegated to the role of simply following instructions. The hard-driving lead buffaloes and their well-intentioned followers suffer the same misfortune as the buffalo on the plains: consistently being outmaneuvered and destroyed by more nimble, sharp-witted competitors.

The newly recommended leadership paradigm is analogized to a flock of geese, which has many leaders flying together in a "V" formation, each knowing where the flock is going. When geese fly in the "V" formation, the entire flock adds significantly more distance to its flying range than if each bird flew alone.

Have you ever noticed a flock of geese flying in formation? One side of the "V" is always longer. Do you know why that is? That side has more geese!

Whenever a goose falls out of formation, it abruptly feels the resistance of trying to fly alone and quickly gets back into line to take advantage of the power of the formation. When the lead goose gets tired, it rotates back in the formation, and another moves into the point position. The back geese honk from behind to exhort those up front to keep up their speed. Finally, when a goose gets sick and falls out of the formation, two geese fall out with it until it is either able to fly or it dies. Then they embark on their own, or with another formation, to catch up with their original group. Now that's dedication to the team!

Rather than being a following herd, you want your team members to emulate a self-directed, interdependent flock of geese. When each person knows the common direction, possesses the skills they need through training and mentoring, is given the opportunity to step into a leadership role, and feels a mutual sense of loyalty from the team, they will take ownership of the team's success.

Practical Application

1. Do you currently have team members who receive preferential treatment in the form of salary or other benefits? Be careful about the message you send to teammates. Regardless of a person's position on the organizational chart, everyone plays an integral part in the success of the team. The sack boy in a grocery store is equally as important as the store manager. The night clerk at a hotel plays as vital a role as the general manager. By treating people with a sense of equality, you will create stronger alliances that play a vital role in your long-term success.

2. Do you currently have a mentoring program in place to develop the skills people need to be promoted to higher levels of pay and responsibility within the team or organization? If not, begin one. Develop potential mentors through train-the-trainer courses and set up a formal program that creates the time and space to make it happen. Allow people to choose career paths based on their interest and enthusiasm.

3. Are people encouraged to "lead up" on your team? Or are they too intimidated or reluctant to speak what's on their

minds? If people are afraid to speak up when they see problems, the team could fall into the trap of groupthink, a stagnated state that may lead to failure. Workers on the front lines of the business are closer to markets and closer to how products are used. Utilize their expertise by adopting a reverse mentoring or "adopt a manager" program where managers work with or "shadow" front line staff people to learn more about the business.

4. Does every individual have a "line of sight" on the overall vision and purpose of the team? Keep people informed through regular team meetings, one-on-one coaching/ mentoring sessions, and written correspondence or e-mail. Ensure that your team emulates a flock of geese rather than a herd of buffalo. *Everyone should be able to drive the bus if called upon to do so.*

Take time during conference calls to have others speak.

Show them how to be GROSS?)

7.

Commit to Playing to Win

*"Freedom is not worth having
if it does not include the freedom to make mistakes."*
—*Mahatma Gandhi*

A number of years ago my son played baseball for a coach who was a nice guy, most of the time, but suffered from Jekyll and Hyde syndrome in the clutch. When his team was winning he was the most positive person around. But when the heat was on and his team was down, he fell apart emotionally and became overly critical, which caused the players to tighten up and begin playing not to lose. After one of their losses, I asked my son what he thought about when he went to bat with his team behind. He said, "I think about what will happen if I strike out."

That same fear runs rampant throughout many organizations today, where employees are thinking about what will happen if they strike out, rather than relishing the thought of hitting a homerun. When people are playing not to lose, they become tense. They refuse to take risks because the consequences of any failed action begin to produce more fear than the prospect of success. This can lead to a vicious cycle of fear-loss-fear-loss-fear-loss.

If you want your team to reach levels of high performance, you must transform those moments of fear and uncertainty into opportunities for ordinary people to achieve extraordinary results.

Don't let them
bring you down.

The late hall-of-fame coaching legend, John Wooden, once told his UCLA basketball team, "Men, the team that makes the most mistakes tonight will win the game!" He encouraged his players to take risks and make more mistakes because he knew that you miss 100 percent of the shots you never take. Wooden was one of the most successful coaches in the history of college basketball because he understood how to create an environment where people play to win.

Rise Above the Naysayers

There was a time in most of our lives when fear had little power over us. There was nothing we couldn't do. No goal was unattainable. We were an unstoppable force of energy that would think of something and then make it happen.

As time passed, the world began to tell us that we cannot do anything we want. Naysayers ridicule our goals and try to discourage us from pursuing our dreams. They say things like, "You can't do that. That will never work. You should play it safe." —Acting as if dreams were meant for others but not for people like us.

Unfortunately this is how many of us go through life, surrounded by people with negative thoughts who try to project their own fears and insecurities on us. Fear begins as a thought and then becomes an emotion that permeates our body and our entire state of being. It can have an infectious grip on both individuals and teams. The negative emotion of fear becomes paralyzing, causing us to play it safe and hold on so tightly to the status quo that we never experience the greatness that is possible.

Don't give naysayers a foothold on your team by allowing them to perpetuate a story of negativity. The story heard is the story told. Tell a different story. One that perpetuates a "play to win" mindset that will allow you to create anything you want. Playing to win requires a commitment that even if you fail, you will never give up and never let your goals and dreams die.

Do you cultivate an environment that is fertile for new ideas on your team? Harness the energy of imagination by encouraging

Fail but learn from it

individuals to risk trying new ideas, even when they don't get off the ground. Remember, the Wright brothers had more than a few crashes before they became airborne. Sure, success has its price. Often it is purchased with great sacrifice, but if everything came easy what would be the real value in succeeding?

To keep a play-to-win attitude, keep your sights fixed on where you want to go. What you give attention to expands. If you focus on what you want, that's what you will attract. If you focus on the things you don't want, guess what appears over and over?

Learn to Fail Forward

The story is told of a time when Thomas J. Watson, the founder of IBM, summoned to his office a young salesman who had recently lost a substantial amount of the company's money in a bungled business transaction. After visiting for some time about what the man had learned from the ordeal, Watson dismissed him to return to work. The young employee was a little surprised. "You're not going to fire me?" he asked. Mr. Watson shook his head and told the young salesman that he had just invested a large sum of money on his education and now the thing to do was to go out and do something with it!

The question is not whether or not people are going to fail, but how they are going to deal with it when they do. Will they fail forward or backward? Listed below are seven abilities of achievers that enable them to fail and keep moving according to John C. Maxwell in his book *Failing Forward: Turning Mistakes into Stepping Stones for Success*:

1. **Achievers Reject Rejection**—People who base their self-worth on their performance often feel dejected and give up when faced with failure. Achievers keep trying because they have an internally based self-image. Rather than say, "I am a failure," they say, "I made a mistake." To keep the right perspective, achievers take responsibility for their actions, but don't internalize failure.

2. **Achievers See Failure As Temporary**—People who personalize failure see a problem as monumental, rather

than momentary, while achievers view their predicament as temporary. People hopelessly quit trying or believing in their potential for success when they view failure as being permanent.

3. **Achievers See Failures As Isolated Incidents**—Achievers refuse to take failure personally. When they fail, they see it as a momentary setback, not a lifelong catastrophe. A single incident will not tarnish their self-image.

4. **Achievers Keep Expectations Realistic**—The greater the accomplishment one pursues, the greater the preparation required to overcome obstacles and keep at it over the long haul. It takes time, effort, and the ability to overcome setbacks. Achievers don't get their feelings hurt when everything doesn't turn out perfectly.

5. **Achievers Focus on Strengths**—Achievers maximize strengths and minimize weaknesses. They keep their attention focused on what they can do, not on what they can't do.

6. **Achievers Vary Approaches to Achievement**—Achievers keep trying and changing until they find something that works for them. They are willing to vary their approaches to problems regardless of the comments or criticism of others.

7. **Achievers Bounce Back**—Achievers have the ability to bounce back after making a mistake. They see life simply as a series of outcomes. Some are what they want, some are not. They learn from each and bounce back. Failure doesn't have to be final.

Playing to win means moving forward regardless of what happens. And that's made possible when people don't take mistakes personally. An event that happened on baseball's opening day in 1954 illustrates this point. The Cincinnati Reds were playing the Milwaukee Braves. Each team fielded a young rookie who was making his major-league debut during the game. The Reds' rookie got hot at the bat and hit four doubles that day to lead his team to a 9-8 victory. The rookie for the Braves had a terrible performance going 0 for 5 at the plate.

The Cincinnati player's name was Greengrass, a name you may not recognize. The name of the Atlanta player, the one who didn't get a hit that day, was Aaron. You've probably heard of him. No doubt he was disappointed, but he didn't think of himself as a failure. He had worked too hard for too long and he wasn't about to give up that easily. And Hank Aaron went on to become the best homerun hitter in the history of baseball!

Focus on winning, rather than losing, and your team will play with confidence and abandon. When the going gets tough, the tough play to win!

Practical Application

1. How does your team react when the going gets tough or they fall behind? Does fear immobilize people? Or are they inspired to perform at higher levels? Build confidence by working up a great game plan. Identify the key results you want to achieve and ensure that each individual has the skills and resources needed to accomplish their specific task(s). Encourage people to take risks and try new ways to accomplish their work.

2. Maximize strengths and minimize weaknesses by focusing on what people do well. Simplify by concentrating on the most important issues, one at a time. Give people permission to have fun, stay loose, and play with enthusiasm. Think positive. Optimism is contagious.

3. Identify what the facts are and remind people that fears are often illusions—products of their own perceptions that serve no useful purpose. Let people know that it is okay to be fearful at times and encourage them to talk through their fears.

8.

Select all types of personalities to make us great.

Commit to Growing Through Adversity

"Adversity has the effect of eliciting talents,
which in prosperous circumstances would have lain dormant."
—Horace

We have become a very impatient and demanding society. No doubt, television plays a huge role in this. On any given night we can tune in and watch as someone's life falls completely apart, then have all the issues resolved and back on track a mere thirty minutes later. Furthermore, computers and the Internet now provide us with immediate access to products, services, and information, which further feeds our appetite for instant gratification.

This may be fine for entertainment purposes, but it is unrealistic when it comes to building work relationships. People have become so accustomed to getting things instantaneously that they often lack the ability to cope when things get messy. Unfortunately, this often results in people giving up, rather than hanging in there and working to figure out solutions to problems. Sadly, by not having the courage or patience to stay the course, they miss a tremendous opportunity to grow. Often, it isn't the good times which build character and bond people together in relationships, but rather the difficult times.

Adversity is a simple fact of life and a necessary ingredient in our development as human beings. To turn away from it is to deny the opportunity to grow, to mature, and to succeed. When everything is going our way and we're experiencing good times, it's easy to be happy and content, but these times are not when strong and lasting relationships are built.

Struggle Produces Strength

One day a man and his young daughter were looking at a butterfly's cocoon when they noticed a small opening on the side. They sat and watched for some time as the butterfly struggled to force its small body through the tiny hole. After a while it seemed to stop making any progress and appeared as if it had gotten as far as it could go. The little girl pleaded with her father to do something, so the man took his fingernail clippers and snipped off the remaining bit of the cocoon. The butterfly then emerged easily, but its body was swollen, and its wings were small and shriveled. They continued to watch the butterfly in hopes that its wings would grow and expand enough to support its body. That didn't happen. The butterfly crawled around with a swollen body and shriveled wings, and eventually died, without ever being able to fly.

Though the man acted out of kindness, he did not understand that the restriction of the cocoon and the struggle required for the butterfly to break free were actually nature's way of forcing fluid from the body of the butterfly into its wings so that it would be ready for flight, once it achieved its freedom from the cocoon. Sometimes struggle is exactly what we need to strengthen us in order to overcome life's obstacles and fly.

Adversity elicits talents and strengths that may have otherwise lain dormant. The greater the challenge the higher you are likely to soar. American literary, Thomas Paine, observed, "The harder the conflict, the more glorious the triumph. What we obtain too cheaply, we esteem too lightly; it is dearness only that gives everything its value. I love the man that can smile in trouble, one that can gather strength from distress and grow brave by reflection. ''Tis the business of little minds to shrink; but he whose heart is

Building a strove team

firm, and whose conscience approves his conduct, will pursue his principles unto death.'"

View adversity as opportunities in work clothes. As a team leader, you will inevitably encounter those who are facing personal challenges. You may have the inclination to jump in and help them out of a jam, but remember the butterfly's struggle to freedom. Sometimes it is better to be a cheerleader who stands by offering words of encouragement, than a rescuer who steps in and cuts away the cocoon. The bumps and bruises that people receive from falling down will often serve to strengthen and enable them to overcome life's obstacles.

Stages of Team Development

High-performing teams do not just form out of the blue. It takes time for a team to develop effectively where all members feel connected to it. Dr. Bruce Tuckman, professor in philosophical, psychological, and comparative studies at Ohio State University, has been credited with identifying four stages that characterize the development of teams. Knowing these stages will help you to understand issues that arise and how to manage adversity more effectively. These four group development stages are known as forming, storming, norming, and performing.

❑ **Stage 1: Forming**—In this first stage, team members possess a high amount of dependence on the leader(s) as they rely on safe, predictable behavior for guidance and direction. Members work to gain acceptance by the team and need to know that they can trust the others. They set about gathering information and impressions about the similarities and differences among their team members as they start to form preferences for future sub-grouping (friendships). Rules of conduct are kept simple to avoid controversy and discussions about serious topics and feelings are avoided. Members endeavor to become oriented to the tasks as well as to each other. Discussions center primarily around defining the scope of the task and how to approach it. To grow from this stage to the next, each team member must surrender the comfort of non-threatening topics and risk the possibility of conflict.

❑ **Stage 2: Storming**—This next stage is characterized by competition and conflict. As team members try to organize for the tasks, conflict inevitably results. Individuals have to bend and blend their ideas, attitudes, feelings, and beliefs to conform to the group standards and expectations. Although conflicts may or may not surface as group issues, they do exist. Questions will arise about who is going to be responsible for what, what the rules are, what the reward system is, and what criteria for evaluation will be. Competition and hostilities emerge over issues of leadership, structure, power, and authority. Because of the discomfort generated during this stage, some members may remain completely silent, others attempt to dominate, and some choose to leave. In order to progress to the next stage, team members must find a way to move from a "testing and proving" mentality to a problem-solving mentality. The most effective tool for helping groups move from this stage to the next is the ability to listen and communicate effectively.

❑ **Stage 3: Norming**—In this stage interpersonal relations become more cohesive. Members have greater understanding and acknowledgment of all teammates' contributions. More focus is placed on community building and solving group issues. Members are willing to let go of personal biases or opinions when presented with facts by other members, and they actively ask questions. Leadership is shared, and cliques begin to disappear. When members begin to know and identify with each other, levels of trust rise, which contributes to a deepening of group unity. It is during this stage that people begin to experience a sense of community and a feeling of contentment as a result of resolving interpersonal conflicts. The most important function of this stage is communication between group members. As they begin to openly share feelings and ideas, give and solicit feedback from one another, and explore actions related to the task, creativity and productivity

It's ok to have conflict. Encourage competition

flourish. If and when this stage of open communication and cohesion is attained by the team, members feel good about being part of the team.

❏ **Stage 4: Performing**—Unfortunately, this stage is not reached by all teams. In order for team members to evolve to this point, they must expand their capacity and depth of interpersonal relationships to encompass true inter-dependence—being able to work independently, in subgroups, or as a total unit, with equal effectiveness. Their roles and authorities dynamically adjust to the changing needs of the team and its individuals. This will be the team's most productive state. Members have become self-assured, and the need for group approval is no longer an issue. Individuals are both highly task-oriented and highly people-oriented. There is harmony, high morale, and loyalty as the team identity emerges. The overall goal is productivity through problem-solving and work, which leads toward optimal team development.

Weathering the Storm

Team conflict is typically seen as negative—scenes of people disagreeing, arguing, yelling, or acting indifferently toward one another. Many leaders avoid dealing openly with conflict because it seems uncomfortable, but these derailments are a normal part of every team's development and functioning. Every team experiences internal conflicts from time to time. Rather than avoid it, you must help your team to deal with conflict head-on to find better solutions and develop a more solid foundation of trust.

Dealing openly with team conflict has a number of benefits for the team and its members:

❏ **Improved clarity and efficiency**—Conflict can help the team to scrutinize and confront possible defects in goals, rules, and procedures.

❏ **Increased productivity**—When managed effectively, conflict helps reduce the amount of time wasted on ineffective processes and procedures.

❏ **Heightened self-awareness and personal development**—
Individuals learn, identify and understand their own
strengths and weaknesses, as well as what is appropriate
and what is not in dealing with conflict.

❏ **Heightened social-awareness and flexibility**—Individuals
learn to understand and appreciate the perspective of others.
This awareness will also help individuals learn how to
anticipate others' concerns and resolve future conflict
situations more smoothly.

❏ **Improved morale and cohesiveness**—When members are
allowed to vent their frustrations, release their tension, and
reduce their stress, they have the potential to reach a greater
understanding of one another's needs and become more
cohesive as a team.

The role of conflict in teams is determined by the manner in
which it is managed. When conflict arises, get the involved
individuals together to discuss and deal with it. <u>Remember to keep
conflict resolution focused on issues, not personalities.</u> Prior to the
meeting, set up some initial ground rules by which each person
involved will engage one another, such as no personal attacks,
name calling, or interrupting others while they are talking. To
ensure that people do not interrupt one another, try utilizing the
traditional Native American Talking Stick ritual. You can use a
stick, a wand, or even a pencil to symbolize the Talking Stick. Only
the person holding the Talking Stick is allowed to speak. Others
must wait their turn to make their own points, argue, agree, or
disagree. This way, all parties involved must take one hundred
percent responsibility for communication, both speaking and
listening.

Use the following format for conducting your conflict
resolution meetings:

1. Let each person state his/her view as objectively as possible.
   Remind him/her to stick with facts, rather than assumptions.

2. Allow any neutral team members present to reflect on areas
   of disagreement.

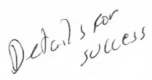
Details for success

3. Explore areas of disagreement to get to the real issue(s). Emphasize priority over personality and the greater purpose to be fulfilled in solving the issues.

4. After identifying the real issue(s), ask each opponent to state what he or she needs to resolve it satisfactorily.

5. If agreement cannot be reached, ask opponents to accept the team's or, in some cases, a mediator's decision for resolution. If an individual refuses to comply then you must help them assess whether or not remaining with the team will be in their and the team's best interest.

6. Once an agreement has been reached, ask opponents for a commitment to "bury the hatchet" and move forward. Explain any consequences that may ensue if they don't.

Sweat the Small Stuff

Few things strike as much fear in the hearts and the bank accounts of homeowners in this country as the tiny termite. Termites account for more property damage each year than hurricanes and tornadoes combined. Ironically, the smallest things can wreak the most havoc in life.

As with termites, it may be little things that are eating away at the foundation of your team. Not big stuff, just little frustrations and annoyances that build day after day. Unfortunately, if you don't deal with these issues in a timely manner, they eventually end up exploding into much bigger problems. It's your choice: You can deal with a little now or put it off and deal with a whole lot later.

Bring your team together regularly to conduct what I call "Sweat the Small Stuff" meetings. During this time, ask members to identify and discuss how to resolve the little issues that they find frustrating or annoying in the work environment. Often, these issues will require little effort to fix, other than to simply bring them to people's attention.

By getting together regularly to discuss the small stuff, your team will become more practiced and skillful in dealing with larger issues, in order to move from the storming stages to the performing stages more timely. You may be pleasantly surprised to find that those issues that once took months to resolve now take weeks...what once took weeks now takes days...what took days now takes hours...and finally what once took hours now takes only minutes to move your team back into the performing stage.

Practical Application

1. Do your team members understand the stages of team development? If not, describe these stages and explain the issues that arise within each. Ask them to assess in what stage they perceive the team is currently. Team members must be aware of the dynamic process of team development. Any time a new member joins the team the stages reoccur.

2. When team members have problems, who can they ask for help? How can you make help more accessible? Whether conflict is internal or external people must have an avenue to bring it into the open. If not, it will fester and grow. If a person has a conflict with another individual on the team they should go to that person or the supervisor, rather than going to others and complaining or discussing it behind their back.

3. Sometimes conflict occurs between a supervisor and a person who is their direct report. How do you allow people to safely bypass the "chain-of-command" when necessary?

4. Set up regular "Sweat the Small Stuff" team meetings. Let people know that the purpose behind these meetings are to identify and resolve the little issues that they find frustrating or annoying. Remind them to bring both problems *and* solutions to the table. These are not intended to be merely gripe sessions. By getting together and talking openly about the small stuff, team members can actually practice the communication and negotiation skills needed for dealing with bigger issues.

I need more Team meetings!

9.

winning is fun

Commit to Having Fun

*"Laughter is the shortest distance
between two people."*
—*Victor Borge*

Having fun at work may be the single most important characteristic of a high-performance team. Research indicates there is a positive correlation between fun on the job and employee productivity, creativity, and morale, as well as customer satisfaction and other factors that determine success. If you want to ensure success for your team, make fun an integral part of your work culture. Or better yet, make it one of your team's core values.

Sadly, some people believe that fun at work is a waste of time or unproductive. That is unequivocally untrue. Humor consultant and author C. W. Metcalf once wrote that "humor is a vital, critical element for human survival, and we often forget about it, and set it aside. We are told that laughter, fun, and play are unadult, unintelligent, and nonprofessional. Nothing could be further from the truth. One of the first indicators of the onset of most mental illness is a loss of a sense of joy in being alive."

Consider how often you laugh on a typical day. Laugh experts tell us that prepubescent children laugh on the average of 110 times per day. As the years pass, the laughter quotient begins to drop drastically, and by the mid-forties, adults typically laugh an average of only eleven times per day. Where did our smiles go between childhood and adulthood?

Having fun on the job plainly creates a healthier work environment. Laughter helps the human body release tension and manage stress efficiently. People cope with change more easily and are more productive under pressure. Organizations who integrate fun into work also have lower levels of absenteeism and downtime, while enjoying higher employee retention and job satisfaction.

Jump Start Creativity

Creativity and fun walk hand in hand according to a study conducted by a team of psychologists at the University of Maryland. Researchers selected two groups of college students who were shown two different videos, then given a range of creative problems to solve. The first group viewed a five-minute film clip of comical bloopers lifted from various sitcoms and weekly television shows. The second group of students watched a math video that was very dry and technical.

As expected, the students in the first group, who had been laughing before the test, fared better at creative problem-solving than the group who watched the math video. But researchers were astonished that the members of the first group proved to be 300 to 500 percent more efficient at problem-solving than their counterparts.

You can increase the power of creativity on your team drastically by permitting people to laugh and have fun before tackling problems. Where there is fun, there is enthusiasm. Where there is enthusiasm, there is energy. And in the presence of energy, creativity abounds.

Understand that all laughter is not the same when it comes to creativity. Laughing *with* someone is much different than laughing *at* someone. The first is a tool for enhancing creativity, while the second produces the opposite effect. Laughing with others is nourishing, supportive, and confidence-building as it brings people closer together in a team spirit of cohesiveness and harmony.

Don't be so serious

Listed below are some simple guidelines to clarify what is not considered to be fun in the workplace:

❏ Fun is not being sarcastic.
❏ Fun is not making fun of, mimicking, or teasing co-workers.
❏ Fun is not telling sexual or ethnic jokes.
❏ Fun is not playing practical jokes or pranks.
❏ Fun is not making fun of the team or organization.
❏ Fun is not being deceptive.

Practice House Rule Number Six

Two prime ministers sat in a room discussing affairs of state. Suddenly a man burst in, enraged with anger, shouting and stomping and banging his fist on the desk. The resident prime minister admonished him: "Peter," he said, "kindly remember House Rule Number Six," whereupon Peter was instantly restored to complete calm, apologized, and withdrew from the room.

The politicians returned to their conversation, only to be interrupted again twenty minutes later by a hysterical woman waving her arms wildly and her hair flying about. Again the intruder was greeted with the words: "Marie, please remember House Rule Number Six." Complete calm descended once more, and she too withdrew with a bow and an apology.

When the scene was repeated for a third time, the visiting prime minister addressed his colleague, "My dear friend, I've seen many things in my life, but never anything as remarkable as this. Would you be willing to share with me the secret of House Rule Number Six?"

"Very simple," replied the resident prime minister. "House Rule Number Six is 'Don't take yourself so g__damned seriously.'" "Ah," said his visitor, "that is a fine rule." After a moment pondering, he inquires, "And what, may I ask, are the other rules?"

"There aren't any," replied his friend.

The message of this story is to—*lighten up*. Fun and laughter are perhaps the best medicine for helping people get over themselves. Lightening up and having fun can bring us together around our inevitable blunders, brain-farts, and communication foibles, and

Laugh @ you (ME).

especially over the ways in which we find ourselves demanding to be taken seriously. *Life is much too serious to take ourselves so seriously!*

Twelve Steps to Fun

Having fun on the job doesn't require extensive training and it doesn't have to be expensive to have a positive impact on every member of your team. Following is a twelve-step program for fun developed by Dave Hemsath and Leslie Yerkes in their book *301 Ways to Have Fun at Work*. They playfully recommend that you read this list daily, poke fun at yourself frequently, and perhaps commit to putting one step a month into action for an entire year.

1. **Start with Yourself**—Don't wait on others to start the fun—become a fun catalyst. Evaluate how you spend your time and decide how you can liven up the spontaneous, fun spirit within yourself and your teammates.

2. **Inspire Fun in Others**—Be a role model for fun. Take risks and don't be afraid to look silly. Give gifts to others that stimulate fun and spontaneity.

3. **Create an Environment that Encourages Fun**—Choose colors that enliven the environment, use music to brighten the mood, and use toys and funny conversation pieces on your desk to relieve stress. Surprise others by frequently changing things around.

4. **Celebrate the Benefits of Fun**—Champion the cause of having fun and its benefits. Be open to others' ideas about creating a workplace that everyone enjoys. Use fun as an excuse to take a break and spontaneously celebrate a job well done.

5. **Eliminate Boundaries and Obstacles that Inhibit Fun**—Fun is contagious. Once you remove the boundaries it will travel fast bringing life and energy into everyone on the team. Don't be afraid to confront people who discourage fun.

6. **Look for the Humor in Your Situation**—People usually want to be around someone who is fun and optimistic, rather than one who is gloomy and pessimistic. Be the person who can find humor in every situation and always be ready to laugh, especially at yourself—remember House Rule Number Six.

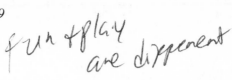
fun + play are different

7. **Follow Your Intuition—Be Spontaneous**—There is no "appropriate" time or place for humor. Don't wait for fun to find you—make it happen when you or others need a boost. The elements of surprise will be refreshing for your work and your work relationships.

8. **Don't Postpone Your Fun**—Fun should not be a reward for completing an assignment. Rather, it is the lubricant for performing well and working effectively with others. Don't put it off; make fun a part of your daily routine.

9. **Make Fun Inclusive**—Fun should be shared by everyone—the more the merrier. When you exclude others, or direct it at them, it ceases to be fun. In fact, humor disguised as sarcasm can be hurtful.

10. **Smile and Laugh a Lot**—Smiling and laughing cost absolutely nothing. They require neither skills nor time to accomplish. Yet they have the most positively contagious impact on your team performance. Greet everyone with a smile and laugh at yourself—others will join you.

11. **Become Known as "Fun Loving"**—If you were arrested for having a sense of humor, would there be enough evidence to convict you? I hope so. One of the greatest compliments you can receive is to be known as a person with a great sense of humor. Make it your personal mission to be the most fun-loving person you know.

12. **Put Fun into Action**—You will be remembered more for what you did than what you said. Grab a fun idea and take action. Have fun every day. Borrow ideas from others or create your own, but most importantly, do it!

Let's make one thing clear when it comes to having fun at work. Fun is not synonymous with "play." The words have two different meanings. When you are having fun you are enjoying yourself. Period! You can be working hard and furious, producing like a maniac, and still be having fun. Play on the other hand, is being engaged in an activity strictly for the sake of enjoyment. It may or may not result in a product; that's not its purpose.

Why is it important to know the difference between the two? Because, too often people mistake fun for play. You may think that if employees are laughing or clowning around at work, it means they are playing. Not necessarily! Sometimes people play at work when they shouldn't and they need to stop it. But energizing, endorphin-flowing fun is a great way to stimulate productivity. *Try it!*

Practical Application

1. Make fun one of your team values. Ask yourself and others each day, "Are we having fun yet?" A fun work environment should be characterized by positive energy and team spirit. If you don't experience that, then you're probably not having fun.
2. Infuse training with fun. When people are having fun they are energized and engaged, which will make them more productive and creative. Get some books on training games and activities that will liven up your training sessions.
3. Make fun the catalyst for productive meetings. How many hours each year do you spend in meetings? People learn and retain information best through interaction and involvement. So take advantage of the opportunity by giving people something to look at, something to listen to, and something to do in order to get the most benefit from meetings.
4. Recognition is a powerful tool to boost performance. Everyone wants to be recognized for something. When efforts to recognize people are mixed with fun it makes the experience even more memorable, as well as motivating people to perform the recognized behavior repeatedly.
5. Build time into the work schedule for recreation activities to help team members keep a "snap in their bow." Be aware of symptoms of burnout, such as apathy, negativity, or exhaustion, and take precautionary actions by awarding time off for people to restore mental, emotional, and physical energy.

Set high Goals.

10.

Commit to Playing Large

"Two roads diverged in a wood, and I—
I took the road less traveled by,
And that has made all the difference."
—Robert Frost

An American businessman was standing at the pier of a small coastal Mexican fishing village when a small boat with just one fisherman docked. Inside the boat were several large yellow fin tuna. The American complimented the man on the quality of his fish and asked how long it took to catch them. He replied, "Only a little while, Señor."

The American asked why he didn't stay out longer and catch more fish. The man said that he had enough to supply his family's immediate needs. The American then asked, "But what do you do with the rest of your time?"

The fisherman said, "I play with my children, take siestas with my wife, and stroll into the village each evening to sip a little wine and play guitar with my amigos. I have a full and busy life, Señor."

The American smiled and said, "I am a Harvard M.B.A. I have a degree in business studies and I could help you. You should spend more time fishing and with the proceeds buy a bigger boat. With the proceeds from the bigger boat you could buy several boats and eventually you could have an entire fleet. Then instead of selling

What are we striving for?

your catch to a middleman, you could sell directly to the processor, and eventually open your own cannery. That way you could control the product, processing and distribution.

"Of course, you would need to leave this small coastal fishing village and move to Mexico City, then Los Angeles, and eventually New York City where you would run your growing enterprise."

The fisherman asked, "But, Señor, how long would all this take?" The American replied, "Fifteen to twenty years."

"But what then, Señor?"

The American laughed, "That's the best part. When the time is right, you sell your stock to the public and become very rich. You'll make millions!"

"Millions, Señor? And then what?"

"Then you can retire and move to a small coastal fishing village where you could sleep late, fish a little, play with your kids, take siestas with your wife, and stroll to the village in the evenings where you could sip wine and play your guitar with your amigos."

With just the hint of a twinkle in his eye, the fisherman said, "Señor, are these business degrees hard to get?"

This story illustrates that those who are driven only by success focus on the bottom line—profitability. Practically all of their knowledge, skills, and time are used to accomplish financial outcomes. Effective? Maybe, for the moment, but what kind of a lasting impact does it really make? Teams who are driven strictly by the bottom line often find themselves plagued by short-term thinking and short-cut techniques that rarely produce the long-term results they desire.

If you want to move your team from being good to great, shift your attention from success to significance. Instead of merely focusing on the bottom line, think about the impact you are making in the lives of your team members, customers, and community.

Teams that play large are concerned with outreach—creating positive change and leaving things better than they found them. When team members are committed to purposeful outreach, they recognize greater value from their work. This increases their sense of commitment to the job and generates better performance and retention. Additionally, the community in which they operate tends

Be Professional!

to view the team more favorably. Like residential neighbors, we respect and admire those we view to be good citizens.

In a similar way, reputation is typically a function of a team's values, which are often expressed in terms of how it conducts business, the way it treats its members, what it gives back to the community, and not merely bottom-line success.

Act Like You've Been There Before

Many people believe that former NFL and Hall-of-Fame running back Barry Sanders was the best to ever pick up a football, and he was certainly one of the most exciting to watch. Beyond his athleticism, he was also one of the most respectful athletes to play any game.

Sander's signature move wasn't dancing or showing off, or pulling a pen out of his sock and signing a football after scoring a touchdown. Instead, it was simply handing the ball to the referee. When asked about his nonchalance after scoring a touchdown, he simply responded, "You have to act like you've been there before."

In today's highly-competitive world there is a simple lesson to be learned from Barry Sander's actions: Skip the showboating! I think it is fine to celebrate a victory or accomplishment. That's not the point here. Celebrating is one thing, but rubbing your opponent's nose in it is something else. There is one thing worse than a poor loser, and that is a poor winner!

Also avoid badmouthing your competition. It will only serve to diminish you—we never make ourselves look bigger by making others look smaller. And it might just motivate your opponent to take their game to another level. In the sports world, that kind of talk is called "bulletin board material." *Do your best and do it with grace and poise!*

Do the Right Things   *Act w/ Integrity*

"It is legal but it was unethical."—Sounds like the mantra for business at all levels these days, doesn't it? Roughly conventional thinking seems to go like this: As long as it is legal, it must be okay. This is not playing large. Instead of simply focusing on doing things right, you must be committed to doing the right things if you want your team to rise from success to significance.

Doing the right thing requires a high degree of transparency and self-disclosure. It means doing away with hidden agendas, manipulation, and dishonesty, and at times allowing the chips to fall where they may. Many are willing to do the right thing when there is no cost involved, but the true test of character is choosing to do the right thing no matter what.

The difficulty sometimes lies in knowing what the right thing is. To help determine whether an action is the right thing, ask the following:

❑ Is it fair?
❑ Is it honest?
❑ Could it hurt anyone?
❑ Would it violate the Golden Rule?—*Do unto others as you would have them do unto you.*
❑ How will we feel about ourselves later if we do it?

Why is it so important to be committed to doing the right thing? There is an old adage that says the world is exactly as you perceive it to be. And perception often stems from and is reinforced by one's own behavior. In other words, we attract that which we are. Someone who is fair and honest will perceive and experience a completely different reality than someone who is self-centered and manipulative.

Plant the Seeds

There is a particular species of the Chinese bamboo tree that, when planted, nothing is seen for four years, other than a tiny shoot protruding meagerly out of the ground. The farmer weeds, waters, cultivates, nurtures, and does all he can to make it successful, but sees nothing. But in the fifth year, this species of the Chinese bamboo tree grows up to eighty feet. In the initial stages all of its growth takes place underground in the root. Then, once a solid root system is in place, all of the growth goes visibly above the ground, giving evidence to the cynics who doubted that growth was taking place along the way.

Doing the right things is highly rewarding, but sometimes you have to plant the seeds and practice patience in reaping a harvest. You must develop a solid root system, a foundation of honesty, accountability and a commitment to do the right things if you want your team to rise from success to significance. This will take time, determination, and the courage to take action. The future depends on what you do in the present. So begin today to plant the seeds that will produce your high-performance team.

Practical Application

1. How do you define success for your team? How do you define significance? If you were to make a shift from success to significance what would it look like? How will significance be measured?
2. Revisit what matters most to your team—your purpose and values. Reevaluate all procedures, processes, and practices to see if they reflect your purpose and values. Are you really walking your talk or are there discrepancies? If so, how will you address them?
3. Are you really committed to being values-driven? When you make choices based on solid values, you will be in a better position to sustain a high level of commitment because you don't have to constantly reassess the importance of what you're doing. Furthermore, a commitment based on something in which you strongly believe is much easier to keep.
4. What does your team stand for? What is your reputation with your customers? What is your reputation in the community? What is your reputation with your competitors? Are you known for being fair and honest? Are you known for doing the right things?
5. What is currently taking place in the area of outreach? Discuss with your team how you can create positive impact in the community and leave things better than you found them.